Lou Gimson is an experienced and accredited business trainer and coach, working with businesses of all types and sizes. She specialises in bringing pre-start entrepreneur's business dreams to reality and has a particular interest in women-owned businesses. She is an accomplished mentor and inspirational speaker.

Lou is a founder member of the charity foundation 'Dream Buddies', which helps individuals to reach their full potential and realise their dreams. As a fellow of the 'Winston Churchill Memorial Trust' Lou is researching female entrepreneurship in the USA.

Allison Mitchell is an inspirational coach, trainer and author. She has spent her entire career in Human Development and is now a pioneer in the field of 'Mum Coaching'. Allison is an NLP Master Practitioner and NLP Coach. She is the founder of Mumcoach and author of *Time Management for Manic Mums*. She believes that with the right attitude anything is possible. To find out more visit; www.mumcoach.com

www.makingit.biz

making it

WOMEN ENTREPRENEURS
REVEAL THEIR SECRETS OF SUCCESS

making it

WOMEN ENTREPRENEURS
REVEAL THEIR SECRETS OF SUCCESS

LOU GIMSON AND ALLISON MITCHELL

CAPSTONE

Other Wiley Editorial Offices

John Wiley & Sons Inc., 111 River Street, Hoboken, NJ 07030, USA

Jossey-Bass, 989 Market Street, San Francisco, CA 94103-1741, USA

Wiley-VCH Verlag GmbH, Boschstr. 12, D-69469 Weinheim, Germany

John Wiley & Sons Australia Ltd, 42 McDougall Street, Milton, Queensland 4064, Australia

John Wiley & Sons (Asia) Pte Ltd, 2 Clementi Loop #02-01, Jin Xing Distripark, Singapore 129809

John Wiley & Sons Canada Ltd, 22 Worcester Road, Etobicoke, Ontario, Canada M9W 1L1

Wiley also publishes its books in a variety of electronic formats. Some content that appears in
print may not be available in electronic books.

A catalogue record for this book is available from the British Library and the Library
of Congress.

Gimson, Lou.
    Making it : women entrepreneurs reveal their secrets of success / Lou Gimson and Allison
Mitchell.
        p. cm.
    ISBN 978-1-84112-700-2 (pbk. : alk. paper)
        1. Businesswomen.   2. Businesswomen—Case studies.   3. Entrepreneurship.
4. Entrepreneurship—Case studies.   5. Women-owned business enterprises.
6. Women-owned business enterprises—Case studies.   7. Success in business.
    I. Mitchell, Allison, 1968-   II. Title.
    HG6054.3.G56   2008
    658.1'1082—dc22

        ISBN 978-1-84112700-2
                                                                    2008031724

Typeset by Macmillan Publishing Solutions
Printed and bound in England by TJ International Ltd, Padstow, Cornwall.

Substantial discounts on bulk quantities of Capstone Books are available to corporations, professional associations and other organizations. For details telephone John Wiley & Sons, Ltd on
(+44) 1243 770441, fax (+44) 1243 770571 or email corporatedevelopment@wiley.com

This book is dedicated to all women who have ever had a dream to create their own business, in the hope that after reading Making It *they are inspired to go for it! Also to my daughters Lauren, Beth and Martha, may you always find the inspiration to follow your dreams.*

'I dream my painting and then paint my dream.' —Vincent Van Gogh

Contents

Acknowledgements

My enormous thanks go to all at Capstone for making this book happen, to my fabulous family and friends for all your support (you know who you are!), my fellow Dream Buddies, with whom I am looking forward to 'sharing the joy', and the many people who have helped me along the way.

A huge thank you goes to all the wonderful women featured in the book for their time, friendship and enthusiasm.

An extra special thanks goes to Allison Mitchell who has given of her time, energy, fun, laughter and all-round amazing attitude to help this book come to fruition.

Permissions List

Page i   Photo taken at Ruby Cottage Arnesby, Leicestershire. Reproduced with thanks to Sarah Salotti.

page 3   "Ac-cent-tchu-ate The Positive" reproduced from Johnny Mercer Song Database (2004), Popular Music Collection, Special Collections Department, Georgia State University Library.

pages 109–110   Go MAD ® is a registered trademark, copyright © Andy Gilbert 2005

List of contributors

Foreword   Emma Harrison – A4e Ltd

Emma Harrison is well known as the charismatic and respected chairman, owner and founder of A4e Ltd. She has succeeded in turning a small regional training provider, founded in 1991, into an international, multi-award winning company. Her philosophy is to 'inspire, encourage and elevate'. Her policy of business diversification has taken the company into new markets that enable the realisation of her overall goal to improving people's lives.

www.A4e.co.uk

1   Steph Cutler – Open Eyed

Open Eyed is a leading influence in the area of disability consultancy in the UK. Founder, Steph Cutler, is a popular writer and professional speaker. Her articles have been published by the BBC, Disability Now! and Handbag.com. She has a commercial background and worked previously in designing, marketing, buying and sales for companies such as Ted Baker and suppliers to Marks and Spencer.

www.openeyed.co.uk
www.making-lemonade.co.uk

2   Josephine LaVey – LaVey Corsetry & Clothing

Josephine designs and manufactures unique corsetry and clothing that caters for all sizes.

Josephine overcame dyslexia and turned around a misspent youth to gain a degree, an award from Prince Charles, and has become a successful businesswoman creating and selling her products around the world. After trading for less than a year, Josephine began to export her original designs. Her business continues to go from strength to strength.

www.laveycorsets.co.uk

3   Sarah Pharo – Pharo Communications

Sarah created a Public Relations company servicing the needs of the agricultural sector, based in Stoneleigh, Warks. She began the company while her family was still young, and built her business to great success. However, she feels she forfeited her family life in the process. Not achieving balance is a regret that she has addressed by spending more time with her grown up daughters and their families. To achieve this she has empowered her staff to make decisions and work with autonomy. Her company has recently expanded into South Africa.

www.pharoweb.co.uk
www.pharoweb.co.za

4   Dawn Gibbins MBE – Flowcrete

Flowcrete began as a partnership between Dawn and her Dad, for a £1 each. Dawn's father devised flooring which could not be eroded by sugar in the garden shed whilst Dawn sold the product to companies such as Mars. Flowcrete is now the world's leading specialist flooring and decking business, backed by a global support network of eight factories and 26 sales offices worldwide. Dawn recently sold the company for millions of pounds.

As Veuve Clicquot Business Woman of the Year, and voted 'Most Influential Person in British Manufacturing', Dawn was the youngest industrialist to be invested with an MBE for Services to UK Industry. A keen Feng Shui practitioner, she has devised a 'barefoot philosophy' which brings a holistic approach to UK lifestyles. She is now known as 'The Barefoot Entrepreneur' and has begun two new businesses.

www.flowcrete.com
www.barefoot-floors.com
www.barefoot-laundry.com

5   Perween Warsi, CBE – S & A Foods

As the founder of one of the UK's most successful food companies, Perween was originally inspired by the need to get better quality Indian food in stores. The company (named after her sons Sadiq and Abid) now employs 900 staff has and a turnover of £65m. It supplies major retailers in the UK and has now expanded into Europe. Perween was awarded an MBE in 1997, followed by a CBE in 2002. She won Woman Entrepreneur of the World Award in 1996, and was given a seat on the Confederation of British Industry's National Committee in 2002. S & A has been the UK's fastest-growing independent food manufacturer for five consecutive years. The company was a finalist in the 1997 Sunday Times Business Awards.

www.sa-foods.com

6   Deirdre Bounds – i-to-i

From stand up comic to founder of i-to-i. When Deirdre founded the ethical travel company i-to-i.com her aim was to challenge traditional ideas in the travel industry. Her company works in partnership with hundreds of locally run projects around the world. The company has grown into an international organization with offices in the UK, USA, Ireland and Australia,  with a worldwide team of 130 passionate, dedicated travel- lovers. i-to-i is now responsible for sending around 5000 people a year to support 500 worthwhile projects in Five continents and also trains a further 15,000 people as TEFL teachers. She has recently sold her company for several million pounds and has created a new role as a motivational speaker.

www.deirdrebounds.com
www.i-to-i.com

7   Karen Wilbourn and Fiona Oxley – Lello

Lello is a UK-based design agency, set up by two sisters based in Leicestershire who create and sell handmade cards in the UK and abroad. They are recent winners of the coveted 'Henries' award. Success to them is the family approach: bringing their sons to work, where they have set up an onsite  crèche facility. They also employ many part-time workers, mainly women on term time contracts, and students. They have fantastic loyalty within their workforce.

www.lelloltd.co.uk

8   Lynne Franks – SEED Women's Enterprise Programme

 Best known as a major figure in PR who ran her own agency from the 1970s to the 1990s. Lynne founded London Fashion Week and started the British Fashion Awards. The character of Edina in the TV series *Absolutely Fabulous* is rumoured to be based on elements of her character. Lynne sold her business when she realised that she didn't like the person she had become and dropped out of the working world to discover who she really was. She returned to business to concentrate on women's issues. In 2004 Lynne adapted her highly successful *The SEED Handbook* (Hay House) into an in-depth training programme to teach entrepreneurial women how to start and sustain a business. The SEED Enterprise Programme is a four-month programme and the first of its kind. SEED is currently being delivered throughout the UK.

www.seednetwork.com

In addition to our model entrepreneurs, as listed on the contributors page, we are grateful to the following individuals and organizations for their assistance in compiling and illustrating this book:

Kelle-Marie Baines and Hayley Carver – Lemon Jelly Arts
www.lemonjellyarts.co.uk

Andy Gilbert – Go MAD® Thinking   www.gomadthinking.com

Bex Knight – Note to Self   www.notetoself.uk.com

Sarah Salotti – Sarah Salotti Photography   www.sarahsalotti.co.uk

Skills for Enterprise   www.skillsforenterprise.co.uk

April Sharpless, ZEST HR Consultancy

Wendy Millington, Average Joes

Fiona Shaw Photography   www.fionashawphotography.com

Foreword

Emma Harrison
Chairman, owner
and founder of A4e Ltd

As a person who began my own company from nothing and built it into a multi-million pound business, I could be considered to have 'made it'.

'Making it' for me is more about what I do and how I do it. My motivation comes from the people that A4E helps to be successful in whatever they choose. We'll do anything that will improve people's lives but more importantly we won't do anything that won't. Satisfaction for me is knowing that we are nurturing others to succeed. Quality is about good health, time spent with my family and friends and making a living doing what I love.

As I have become financially secure I am able to share what I have learnt and mentor others to create the business of their dreams. My passion is inspiring and helping others to find their way.

This book uniquely shows you how to turn your ideas into reality and shares with you the wealth of experience behind the stories.

So get reading and look forward to your own success, remember it's you that defines it, enjoy!

With my very best wishes

Emma

Emma Harrison is a well-known, charismatic and respected entrepreneur and the Chairman, owner and founder of A4e Ltd.

Emma has a unique approach to leadership, seeing her role as being to 'Inspire, encourage and elevate'. It is this business philosophy that has seen her turn a small regional training provider, founded in 1991, into an international, multi-award winning company. Furthermore Emma has built a company that follows her principle of 'doing well by doing good' and has implemented a policy of business diversification that has taken the company into new markets that enable it to realise its overall goal of improving people's lives.

Emma is 42 and lives at Thornbridge Hall in Derbyshire with her husband Jim and her young family.

Introduction

Why is it that some women create fabulous businesses, are financially independent and generally live the life of their dreams, while others sit on the sofa watching television and thinking how life could have been *if only*?

- *If only* I had a brilliant idea
- *If only* I had the confidence
- *If only* I'd been to business school
- *If only* I had a degree
- *If only* I had more time
- *If only* I had more support
- *If only* I was more talented

Are you a woman who has aspirations to own a business? Let's make sure that doesn't remain just a dream. Read on to ensure you are equipped with exactly the right attitude to go for it! The famous women entrepreneurs of today all started somewhere. What you may not realize is that there are many women out there just like you, who do own a business and are living their dreams, successfully juggling their family and work lives and feeling fulfilled. You may not want to be famous or to own an empire – you may want to be responsible for your own destiny and to do something you love to create an income. Wherever you want to position yourself in business, we are here to help you by inspiring you to live your life as you choose and to have no regrets.

When I first began working for myself I thought I was prepared. I took it upon myself to learn all about the practical side of running a business, made sure I was operating on the right side of the law and learnt how to do my own bookkeeping and so on. What I wasn't expecting were the emotional hurdles I had to jump over all the time. I firmly believe that if you couple the right attitude with the correct practical knowledge, success is waiting to happen.

I wanted to find out how other women had reached success and how they define it for themselves. It's easy to think that success is measured only in financial terms, but that isn't the case. *Making It* is a compilation of inspirational women's true stories, sharing with you how they started their businesses and how they overcame hurdles to reach success. The definition of 'success' may be a financial measure, or more of a value measure like spending lots of time with their families, being in charge of their own destiny, or making a difference with what their business does. The book is also a story of networking, something women do naturally. I have found that as I have shared my dreams of turning the book into reality and told people about its purpose, they in turn have told other people so that contacts and women to interview have come to me quite easily – the power of networking!

What astounds me are the amazing attitudes of the women I have interviewed. To be successful you need to adopt the right attitude. My aim is for you, the reader, to resonate with the qualities these women have and realize that you too possess the same qualities.

Visit our website www.makingit.biz for help, advice, inspiration and information. We hope we can enable you to score highly on our 'attitude-O-meter', thoroughly enjoy your business journey, and we'd love to hear your own stories. You have a choice, you can use the guidance in this book and you can make it too!

Accentuate the positive

You've got to accentuate the positive,
Eliminate the negative,
Latch on to the affirmative,
Don't mess with Mister In-Between.

Johnny Mercer

The first questions to ask yourself when considering creating your enterprise are: What am I good at? What do I love doing?

If you earn a living doing something you are good at and you love doing, it won't feel like work. How exciting does that sound? Do you look forward to Monday mornings? I am privileged to work with many people who do. People just like you who are embarking on their new business journey. The people who turn out to be successful pay equal attention to what they are not so good at and look at finding solutions to overcome their weaknesses.

Mentoring Moments

I am working with a relatively new drama company operating in both London and the Midlands called Lemon Jelly Arts. The two founders,

Hayley Carver and Kelle Baines, have an excellent pedigree in both dance and drama training and experience. Their workshops and academies are second to none, drawing on their own professionalism and their experience. They are building up a fabulous reputation for themselves. However, this wasn't always the story.

When I first met them they had just changed their name as their previous one was too similar to another company's. They had failed to check this out first; all their early efforts of building up a reputation had to stop as they were threatened with legal action. Hayley and Kelle also had an 'all singing all dancing' business plan that looked very professional, the only problem being that it was tucked away in a drawer and neither of them understood it fully or used it as a working document to help them grow and flourish. They also knew they had money in their business account, so cash flow was good, although they avoided looking at the full financial picture.

Fortunately, they recognized that their strengths were exactly what were needed to build their business and that their weaknesses could be overcome if they asked the right people for help. They arrived at Skills for Enterprise offices with a new business name that they had checked wasn't already being used and had registered with both Companies House and the HMRC – great, first problem solved. The next step was to create a viable business plan that they both agreed to take the business to where they wanted it to be.

Hayley and Kelle are two very creative people, so I took them through a visualization exercise in order for them to see, hear and feel what success meant to them. This was immediately put on to a huge piece of paper in the form of a mind map with pictures and words. We then turned it into an umbrella business plan (see Chapter 5). This seemed to be a real breakthrough, as they could get all the finer details down while remaining focused on the bigger picture. At the end of this exercise there was a plan in place to help them to drive their business forward. They didn't need to borrow any money, so a formal business plan wasn't even necessary.

The next stage was to look at the finances. Hayley and Kelle were surprised at the healthy financial position Lemon Jelly Arts was in. They were making things hard for themselves by not using easier methods of payment and recording information. I encouraged them to make an appointment with their accountant to sort these issues out. The end result was that Hayley and Kelle can now get on with doing what they do best: teaching children to be fabulous thespians, improving their self-confidence and generally helping the next generation of adults to accentuate the positive!

How about doing this kind of exercise for yourself? A good tip is to be completely honest.

First, make a list of all your personal strengths, for example 'I am a great communicator', 'I am focused'. Ensure that the statements are in the present tense and repeat them to yourself often. I've included five spaces in the list below – make sure you complete at least three.

Strength 1................................Exploit..............................

Strength 2................................Exploit..............................

Strength 3................................Exploit..............................

Strength 4................................Exploit..............................

Strength 5................................Exploit..............................

Take your list of strengths and work out how you are going to exploit them to help your business.

Now it's time to look at your weaknesses. Complete the list below as you did with your strengths, ensuring that you use statements in the present tense and fill in at least three weaknesses.

Weakness 1............................Overcome...........................

Weakness 2............................Overcome...........................

Weakness 3............................Overcome...........................

Weakness 4............................Overcome...........................

Weakness 5............................Overcome...........................

Take your list of weaknesses and decide how you are going to overcome them.

It is also a wise move to compare the strengths and weaknesses of your competitors. While it is bad practice to point out your competitors' weaknesses to potential customers, knowing them yourself means you can take advantage of them.

Fill in the chart below as fully as you can.

Once you have a full picture of what your competitors are doing it is easier to make your own business decisions.

For example, if you own a small grocer's shop you aren't going to be able to compete using the same strengths as the major supermarkets. Asda, Tesco and Sainsbury's are all able to:

• Compete on price.
• Afford expensive advertising campaigns.
• Have celebrities endorse their brand.

Competitors' strengths and weaknesses

Top three competitors Name, address etc.	Strengths	Weaknesses
Competitor 1:		
Competitor 2:		
Competitor 3:		

Focus on their weaknesses instead:

- Their stores are large so it takes time to park.
- They are busy so it takes longer to shop.
- They are possibly not close by.

Therefore, the strengths of your small grocer's could be:

- Convenience.
- Personal service.
- Ordering in speciality goods for customers.
- A community feel.

It's now time to exploit your business strengths in your marketing. Good luck!

Entrepreneur's Experience

I personally have always loathed doing the day-to-day record keep-ing side of business. I procrastinate, always putting it off. It's not that I can't do it; it is because I would rather be doing far more exciting things, like winning the next client. I chose to ignore this major weak-ness and as I result I never knew where I was financially from month to month. I kept the information in my head, this was there in the background all of the time and it became very stressful.

When it was time to fill in my tax return I knew I had to apply myself and just do it. I laid out a year's worth of receipts on my conservatory floor in month order, ready to collate. The phone rang – as I got up to answer it the conservatory door opened slightly and the receipts blew everywhere. I had to start over again. It was at that point I vowed to sort the weakness out.

I contacted several accountants and found one who was reasonably priced and would do everything for me. All I had to do was put my receipts and invoices in an envelope at the end of each month, send them to him and by return I received a set of monthly management accounts.

I now feel confident in the knowledge that everything is in order. My financial situation takes minutes to review. I can spend my time win-ning more business and as a result I'm earning more money.

As a working mum, this experience made me look at other jobs I did that I could 'outsource'. Cleaning my house and ironing my family's clothes were again jobs that I endured. Using the word 'outsourcing' and looking at it in a business way made me drop the guilt I had pre-viously attached to my thinking. I could earn far more per hour than I was paying my domestic help, and I was also helping another local business do what they did best: clean! I was beginning to accentuate the positive and eliminate the negative. How refreshing!

Making It – Meeting Steph Cutler, Open Eyed

I had been asked to give a presentation and workshop as part of Enterprise Week with the subject 'The Big Idea'. This was to help potential entrepreneurs to think creatively and come up with their own big idea that was to make them lots of dosh. Well, not one who is shy at such a request, I said yes and set about making some notes.

It wasn't until the programme of events was emailed through to me that I realized it was an event aimed at people with varied disabilities. 'What's the problem with that?' I hear you thinking. No problem – except it completely threw me out of my comfort zone. I have experience in dealing with people with various disabilities on a one-to-one basis. Talking to an audience of 70 with hearing, sight, physical and mental disabilities scared me silly. I was so afraid of offending anyone that I knew I was in danger of offending everyone! My usual patter while 'warming up' my audience and putting them at ease includes such statements as 'Can you hear me at the back?' 'Can everyone see the flipchart and screen?' Clearly, I couldn't use these phrases and I knew I had to be careful of the language I did use.

Before the presentations began I was called to a meeting with the signers who were there to assist the audience. On the paperwork I had been sent there was a typing error and it read 'singers' – I had felt sure that it wasn't *The X Factor*!

Meeting over, the presentations began. Centre stage was Steph Cutler from Open Eyed, a disability and training awareness company that she had formed after experiencing her own sight loss. How I wished there was time for me to have a conversation with her before I began my workshop with the 70-strong audience for some tips in addressing them. What I heard next was one of the most inspirational stories about how a business came to be. I could feel the hairs stand up on the back of my neck as her story unfolded. I knew immediately that her message had to get to a wider audience and with her permission Allison and I interviewed Steph about her incredible start in business ownership, her definition of success and her tips for business. Steph has given us permission to use the very speech she made at that event, entitled 'Making Lemonade'. I feel that no one can tell this better than she can herself.

For those of you interested, my workshop went down well. I had a couple of 'Bridget Jones' moments but nothing too bad, and for those people we are continuing to help to set up their businesses I shall look to Open Eyed for advice!

Making Lemonade – Steph Cutler's Story

'Less than three years ago I was a successful fashion designer working hard and playing hard in London. I was designing for the likes of Ted Baker and Marks & Spencer.

'It was while on holiday that I made a discovery. I was in New Zealand and on the way back from a sightseeing trip we stopped off at an amusement park called Puzzling World. One room was made up of optical illusions. I followed the instructions and I stared at a wall with black vertical lines with my left eye closed and then repeated the exercise with my right eye closed. The lines were supposed to change thickness or something. But with my right eye closed I couldn't see the lines at all. That's pretty clever, I thought. A bit blonde!

'However, when I got back into the car I tried again and I still couldn't see well through my left eye. I was not overly worried, I was having fun on holiday and thought I should go to the opticians on my return.

'Eventually I found the time and went along to an optician in my lunch hour. She covered my left eye and I read the whole lettered chart right down to the bottom line without any problem. She covered my other eye and I couldn't see the chart at all. She advised me to go to the eye hospital right away, which I did. At the hospital no one could tell me what was wrong with my eye and it was decided I would need to see a consultant.

'That evening I was casually recounting my day to my parents. For me there were no real alarm bells ringing, but unbeknown to me the alarm bells on my parent's end of the phone line were deafening.

'The next day I was getting ready to go to work when I opened my door to my parents. Considering they live in Coventry and I lived in London, I was not expecting to see them. They came in and broke down and told me I was going to go blind! I think I must be the only person ever to take this news with relief. Seeing my parents in such a state I assumed something terrible had happened to my sister, who was at the time on honeymoon in Australia. I found myself comforting them and I was very English and made them a cup of tea.

'We spent the morning at the hospital, I had lots of tests and while it wasn't officially diagnosed, my symptoms and family history meant it was clear I had a condition called Lebers Optic Neuropathy. I decided that until it was confirmed I wasn't going to worry about it and I went back to work.

'The following week it was confirmed to me that I had three months with full vision and then my second eye would deteriorate and then I would have no central vision. My consultant broke the news in a nonchalant kind of way. I was grateful to him for this, as it played a big part in how I took the news. I did not know what central vision loss would mean to me practically or emotionally, but I made a very conscious decision there and then in the hospital that this would not mean the end in any way for me and I made a vow to myself that I would keep to this.

'Despite loving my job, I did not fancy spending the last few months with full sight looking at the four walls of work and so I took myself off to see some of the world while I could. It is an odd feeling to be taking photos that you don't know you are going to be able to see on your return.

'The three months were coming up and I would wake up every morning and would tentatively open my eyes to see if I could still see, but my good eye remained good. I started to actually will it to happen. Think about it: how long do you give something like that? I'd left my job and there was never any talk of it not happening. My view was that as soon as it happens, the sooner I can deal with it. No one could explain why it hadn't happened and suggested that it might not happen at all.

'I put together a great portfolio and got myself a fab new job, designing for Next. It was a promotion, pay rise, lots of travelling and working on a good range. I moved back to London and started on the Monday and realized that I couldn't see my computer screen or the artwork. It was fair to say the timing was cruel and I left on the Friday.

'Central vision loss did of course affect me practically. As I retained my peripheral vision, my mobility isn't affected. I can make out most things so I don't bump into objects. I can't read, see my computer screen, see colour well, see fine detail or make people out easily – and for any of you men out there thinking of telling me you look like Brad Pitt, don't bother!

'Emotionally I stayed strong. From day one I eliminated the word 'can't' from my vocabulary and set goals. Over the last couple of years I have personally experienced the incredible effect this has. If you tell yourself you can't do something then you probably can't. That is because you are feeding your brain a message that it is not possible.

'*If* you send your brain a message that you *can* do something then you no doubt can. Convince yourself that it is possible and your whole mindset will be positive and your goal will be achievable. Providing you work hard and effectively towards it, and never lose sight of the fact you can do it, it will be achieved.

'My goal was to get my life back to what it was. I believe anything is possible, but I also believe that sometimes you can't do everything by yourself. The desire has to come from you, but I believe you should never let your pride be an obstacle.

'I am eternally indebted to my family and friends. With the best will in the world, when you are thrown from a familiar sighted world to an unfamiliar visually impaired world there is a lot to learn. Trouble is, all usual avenues of learning are not available. Printed material and the internet are not immediately accessible. Therefore being too proud to ask for help will get you nowhere fast.

'I decided from day one that sitting at home learning to live with my limited vision would not help me learn to live with my limited vision. I forced myself to go out and about. I put myself on the train and came back down to London to visit my friends. It was practically difficult and emotionally hard to see my friends who were living my old lifestyle, doing my old job and earning the money I used to earn. I believe if something scares you, you should give it a go and this was definitely the right approach for me. The more I pushed myself the easier it became.

'I was put in touch with a college in Birmingham that specialized in helping visually impaired people. It was with great trepidation that I turned up on my first day. I had no idea how they could help, I just knew they had to as I had no plan B. I told this to everyone I met and at the end of the assessment it was decided they could help.

'The problem was, the course was six weeks long and there were only four weeks left before the college closed for the summer. The more intuitive among you will have realized that I am not particularly patient. There was no way I could wait until September to start to get back to normal. I think they really were too scared to turn me away, as by the end of the day it was agreed they would keep the college open for a further two weeks in order for me to complete the course.

'I have never worked so hard. I was learning how to use a computer again but with a screen reader. I couldn't use a mouse as I couldn't see where to click and I had to learn how to do everything differently and without seeing the screen.

'By the end of the summer – the time I would have only just been starting had I not scared the college – I had reached my first goal. I was employable again.

'Along the way, as my sight had gone through the deterioration phase, I had to concede that I couldn't return to my career in fashion design. It is a very visual job and a very impatient industry. Tomorrow is always too late and even with sight it was difficult at times. It was a hard blow to take, but there were plenty of other things I knew I could do well. I had a great track record, transferable skills, a good CV and was enthusiastic – but none of this, it seemed, counted for anything if I didn't have full sight.

'Up until this point I had remained positive despite leaving behind my career, friends, lifestyle and living with limited vision. Having worked so hard and endlessly filled out application forms I couldn't see with no response at all. I started to become despondent. This was my next goal and there was nothing more I could do than I was doing. I am not superhuman and my resolve started to fade.

'There is one major factor which meant I did not fall into a depressive state and that was that I knew I could do it. It was all the employers that assumed I couldn't and I knew they were wrong. About 18 months ago I decided to stick a big two fingers up to all those employers and I employed myself.

'While living with my acquired disability, I experienced the fact that many of the barriers disabled people face are created by non-disabled people's lack of awareness. On one of the occasions when I had forced myself to come down to London, I had asked a London Underground worker for some assistance. He helped me very appropriately and on chatting to him I discovered he was able to support sensitively because he had had visual awareness training. At the time I wondered if there was anything in this, but I was still in my rehabilitation period.

'I set up my own Disability Equality Consultancy and I use my personal experience and knowledge to help organizations make their services accessible to everyone. I have had the benefit of a disabled and non-disabled person's perspective and as a business owner I believe passionately in the business case for inclusion and accessibility.

'I have not looked back since setting up my consultancy. I still have outstanding goals, but I am well on my way. As you can imagine I have learned a lot in the last few years and one saying has stayed with me throughout and that is: "If in life you are dealt lemons, then make lemonade."'

Strengths and weaknesses

Steph identifies her own strengths and weaknesses something like this:

Personal strengths

- Ambitious
- Clear
- Structured goal setting

After losing her sight, as it enhanced a few things, she became

- More organized
- Adaptable
- Determined

Personal weaknesses

- Impatient
- Likes other people to be passionate and committed

Business strengths

- Sector specific
- Approachable
- Put customers at ease
- Human face
- Enthusiastic
- Makes it happen

Business weaknesses

- Numbers! Steph overcomes this by outsourcing her accounts
- Steph also has an assistant for 15 hours per week that is paid for by a government scheme called Access to Work. This is crucial to Steph and gives her someone to drive and read for her.

During the course of our interview it became apparent that Steph's lemonade bottle is firmly half full. When she is having a bad day she allows a maximum of 24 hours to wallow, then it's business as usual. She also looks at who is having a better day than her instead of who is worse off. On one of her 'bad' days she saw a girl being proposed to on a bridge and shifted her thoughts to how the girl must be feeling.

Steph's business achievements have made the national finals in three business awards:

- *Enterprising Young Brit 2006.* Steph was short listed for the Social & Environmental category of the *Daily Mail* Enterprising Young Brits competition 2006 with her joint business, Image Intelligence. This image consultancy designed specifically to be accessible to visually impaired people appealed to the judges, who included representatives from HM Treasury, the Daily Mail, Lloyds TSB and celebrity judges Kanya King, founder of the MOBO awards and Margherita Taylor, Capital Radio DJ and television presenter. In attendance at the awards luncheon was the Rt Hon Gordon Brown, then Chancellor of the Exchequer.
- *Barclays Trading Places Awards 2006.* Open Eyed beat hundreds of applicants to be one of ten finalists to attend a glittering gala awards dinner at London's Café Royal. The Trading Places award is a unique tribute to people who have turned their lives around by starting a successful business. The awards are sponsored by Barclays, backed by government and endorsed by a host of celebrity entrepreneurs, including the late Dame Anita Roddick, Sir Terence Conran, Simon Woodroffe, Bill Wyman and Lord Sainsbury.
- *Handbag.com and Barclays Business Plan Awards 2005.* After impressing judges with her comprehensive business plan to set up

Steph's top tips

- Don't let your pride prevent you from becoming successful. Accept support and ask for it if it will move your business forward.
- Talk to everyone passionately like they want what you do. Don't make assumptions about who your customers are: you don't know who they know or what their plans are.
- Don't work to your business plan like it is set in stone. Keep an open mind and be prepared to adapt to new opportunities.
- Set realistic, short-term goals and monitor your progress. From time to time look back at how far you have come and acknowledge your achievements.
- Work hard to maintain your business relationships. People's circumstances and requirements change.
- Continue marketing even when your diary is full.
- Give yourself a break. Taking time out for a facial, round of golf or shopping trip is time well spent. You will return to your business with a clear head.
- Ask your customers why they use you. It's the best way to find out how to retain them and how to sell to potential customers.
- Read about and listen to other successful people, be inspired by them and learn from their experiences.
- Understand that you can't be good at everything. Excel at what you are great at and create strategies to deal with your weaknesses, outsourcing them if possible.

Open Eyed, Steph reached the finals in the 2005 handbag.com and Barclays Business Plan Awards. Open Eyed was acknowledged at the final held at an awards ceremony at renowned Conran restaurant Sartoria, attended by the cream of Britain's successful businesswomen including Sahar Hashemi, co-founder of Coffee Republic, and Nicola Gerwitz, founder of Lola Rose.

Steph is very willing to share her secrets of success with you in the form of her 'top tips' and her experiences of networking (go to www.openeyed.co.uk or www.making-lemonade.co.uk).

Networking, networking, networking

'Networking, Networking, Networking! is the business equivalent of the political mantra Education, Education, Education. It is the key to business start-up, business sustainability and business development.

'While sitting in front of a grant-awarding panel recently, one of the panellists commented on the size of the entertainment expenditure on my cash-flow projections. "What can I say?", I said. "I am a very sociable person!" I love to meet people. It is by listening to others that I learn everything from how best to promote a service to how not to behave. These things may make me approachable, likeable and good company, but they do not necessarily make me a good networker.

'Networking events organized to provide networking opportunities may suit some people, but I think there is an art to networking at these events. To be a good networker you need to plan your time and work the room with military precision. You need to approach strangers boldly, strike up a conversation, quickly ascertain whether there is potential for business, and be able to retreat to the next stranger if there is not.

'So, despite being a confident communicator and being able to talk credibly and with enthusiasm about my business, I struggle at these events. I find myself gravitating towards the buffet and comfort eating to ease the pain. This, I know, is more likely to increase my dress size than my client base!

'I struggle for another reason: I am visually impaired. What this means practically is that I can't see the delegates list; I can't see your name badge; and I can't see very well what's on the buffet I can be found propping up. I do not *look* visually impaired. In fact, I can walk up to you, make conversation and you would be none the wiser; which, in itself, is part of what makes attending a struggle. I don't know who I am talking to. I therefore can't identify attendees I would particularly like to speak with, and not only that, but I sometimes struggle to identify who I have just spoken to.

'In for a penny, in for a pound. I rock on up to fellow attendees and introduce myself and ask their name, at which point they will more often than not point to their name badge, but I am none the wiser. I then have to decide whether to continue while being unsure of who they are and what they do, which is tempting but not ideal, or explain that I can't see the badge. The latter approach can have a number of different responses, which mostly end in the same result. "Have you forgotten your glasses?" tends to mean merely that getting to the awkward silence takes a little longer and can be a bit more awkward, when I have no choice but to explain gently that I am actually registered blind. Telling them of my acquired sight loss does at least have the advantage of introducing my disability awareness consultancy into the conversation.

'At my first networking event, I came horribly close to passing my empty plate to a fellow delegate, mistaking him for a waiter! Suppressing the urge to burst into laughter at my near "Bridget Jones" moment was made no easier as I then found myself seated next to the waiter lookalike for the rest of the evening!

'The last networking event I attended was a breakfast meeting with an unsociably early start. On arrival, I pinned on my name badge. The company name read "Open Eyed", but the wearer was anything but. Had I known the company of some middle-class, middle-aged men in suits beckoned, I would have stayed under my duvet!

'I replied to one of the aforementioned, telling him that I own a disability awareness consultancy. On hearing this he proceeded to tell me how ridiculous it was that disabled people should want to be able to access services. Even more "ridiculous" was the fact that he had been forced to install a disabled toilet in his building. With increasing incredulity, he went on to say that nobody disabled would ever use it because the entrance to his building was not wide enough to fit a wheelchair through. I agreed that was "ridiculous", but we were poles apart with our reasons. I considered saying I hoped he wouldn't have an accident on his way home as, if he found himself required to use a wheelchair, he would not be able to get into his office to use his expensive toilet, but I refrained. The name badge routine hadn't occurred and so he was unaware of my sight loss and I was therefore blissfully unaware of his name.

'I then met Mr Small Town CV Consultant. He asked me what I did and he responded with "That's nice", then laughing he continued, "but come on, would you really put that you were disabled on your CV?" To this, I smiled and said, "I am and I do", but this went right over his balding head. Mr Disabled Toilet and Mr Small Town CV Consultant shared the love of the sound of their own voices, while making nonsensical and insensitive points. I asked the latter to consider that the person who, at the time, arguably held one of the most powerful jobs in the country was totally blind. I left him to ponder David Blunkett's CV dilemma and made a beeline for the buffet!'

Making It Happen for You – Accentuate the Positive

What did Steph do?

- Created a positive here and now.
- Sought out the positive aspects in negative situations.
- Fully expected a positive future.

How can you model Steph and accentuate the positive?

- Always assess your current situation in a positive way.
- Learn how to turn negatives into positives.
- Set positive expectations for your future.

How much do you accentuate the positive?

Think about what you really want to achieve in your business. With that in mind, score yourself from 1 to 10 on the statements below. A score of 0 means you really disagree and a score of 10 means you really agree.

- When I wake up, I think about all the good things that will happen in the day ahead.
- If things go wrong I can usually see the funny side.
- If I'm in a group of people who are moaning I will tend to turn the conversation to something more positive.
- I believe that things usually turn out all right.
- I have a voice in my head that encourages me and tends to be positive.
- I usually see the best in people.
- I expect things to go well.
- People see me as a positive person.

- Faced with a problem I think more about solutions than who is to blame.
- There's no such thing as failure.

CHECK YOUR ATTITUDE

Add up your total score out of 100.

- *If you scored 85–100 points* – You have a very positive disposition. Use the exercises below to be positively sure you're not missing any other opportunities to be even more positive.
- *If you scored 50–84 points* – You can be a little negative at times. Take some positive action to increase your score.
- *If you scored 0–49 points* – You probably have a lot of negativity. Work on building your positivity muscle.

Three Steps to Accentuating the Positive

A positive, optimistic attitude is one of the true attributes of winning entrepreneurs. Steph most certainly has one and it's been shown time and time again that in business, people who see the glass as half full rather than half empty usually do better.

The half-empty, half-full debate always reminds me of a story I once heard Robert Dilts tell about conjoined twins. Despite the fact that they were born at the same time, in the same place and, by virtue of the fact that they were joined at the hip, raised in exactly the same way, they viewed life quite differently. For the first few years of their life things didn't go too well for them, they had many operations and it was often touch and go if they would survive, but they did pull through. In their early childhood things improved for a while as their health stabilized. At age 8, life deteriorated again. Their parents divorced, partly due to the strain of bringing up the twins. After a rough patch of adjustment to this, life became good again as they settled into a lovely new neighbourhood, with just their mother to bring them up.

One day twin one said to twin two, 'Isn't it great how things always work out fine in the end?'

Twin two looked surprised and replied, 'How can you say that when you know that things always get worse just after they get better?'

The question is, which of the twins is right? They both are, but they've chosen to experience and interpret what's going on in their individual worlds in a different way. One twin processes information positively, the other negatively. Those of us who tend to be more positive and optimistic perceive the world like the first twin, in a positive way. We look for and accentuate the positive. Those of us who are negative tend to do the opposite. Like the second twin, we have a tendency to find the negatives in situations. It's a bit like wearing a pair of tinted sunglasses in the summer. The lenses filter out the light that you don't want in your eyes and the tint makes everything look slightly different to how it really is. The sky might look duller, the grass more yellow. In truth, the grass and the sky are exactly the same colour they've always been – you just see them differently when you put on your glasses.

This different view of the world is not a reflection of reality. It's a reflection of what is being filtered in and out. If you want to accentuate the positive you've got to filter for it and consciously let it in. Follow the three steps below to accentuate the positive and eliminate the negative.

STEP 1: ALWAYS SEE YOUR CURRENT SITUATION IN A POSITIVE WAY

Use the positivity toolkit to filter for the good things in your life.

Positivity toolkit: Get new glasses and filter for the positive

I once saw a hypnosis show, in which the hypnotist told his willing volunteer that she was wearing a pair of magic spectacles. He told her that everybody she looked at through these specs would appear to her to be completely naked. Despite the fact that everybody in the audience was fully clothed, it became obvious very quickly that to this person everybody did look naked. Isn't it amazing how we can create a reality for ourselves? Even though no one else could see naked people, this woman absolutely believed that she could.

You too can use this technique to your advantage. Each day when you get up, imagine that you are putting on a pair of imaginary glasses. Don't get too excited, you won't be filtering for nakedness! Through these glasses you can only see positive things, you can only interpret things in a positive way. The glasses will help you to filter your world so that you actively look to accentuate the positive in events. When you take off your imaginary glasses at night, mentally tick off in your mind five great things that happened to you that day.

Train your brain to accentuate the positive. The more you exercise your positivity muscle, the bigger it will get. The less you dwell on negatives, the more your negativity muscle will shrink. The more you do this, the more you'll enjoy it. The world does look good when you choose to perceive it positively.

In her story Steph constantly accentuates the positive. Although she is losing her sight and working as a top fashion designer is no longer viable, she is still able to put a positive spin on her situation. It's as if she sees everything through a pair of rose-tinted positivity specs. She says things like 'I absolutely knew I could do it', 'From day one I eliminated the word "can't" from my vocabulary'.

Positivity toolkit: Stop negative thoughts in their tracks

This is a very effective way of distracting yourself from any negative thoughts. If a negative voice should somehow manage to get through your filter and into your head, try this technique to distract the voice and make it more positively focused.

Choose a method to distract yourself: pinch yourself, clap your hands, say 'no' to yourself, wear an elastic band on your wrist and flick it. The choices are endless, but be aware of what you choose if it's something you are likely to have to do in a public place! (Slapping yourself hard across the face might not be exactly the right thing to do as a negative thought enters your mind.) When the negative thought manifests itself, activate your method of distraction, for example pinching yourself or clapping your hands, and at the same time say to yourself: 'I am no longer like that, I accentuate the positive.'

Positivity toolkit: Get positive about your life
Make a point of dwelling on all the great things that have ever happened to you in your life. Create something that celebrates the positive aspects of your life and all your achievements to date. Be creative: it could be a collage of photos, a list, or a laminated card. I once met a woman who had put all her great achievements onto a t-shirt. When she was feeling negative she put it on to change her mood. Whatever

your choice is, consult it often and keep it alive. Let it grow it by adding new positive events to it, events that will accentuate the positive nature of your life right now.

STEP 2: LEARN HOW TO TURN NEGATIVES INTO POSITIVES

Steph is very good at taking what many people would see as negatives and viewing them as positives. A technique to help you do this is reframing, or how to find a silver lining in any hideous situation! Here's how you do it.

Take an unfavourable situation and reframe it by looking for the opportunities in it. Steph encapsulates the idea of reframing beautifully when she says:

'In life if you are dealt lemons, then make lemonade.' In other words, take the negatives but focus on how you can turn them into positives. She's certainly taken a spoonful of her own medicine in seeing her disability in a positive light, as it's given her another perspective on the world that has helped her to create her own thriving business.

Being able to reframe disadvantages or setbacks as possible opportunities is a useful business skill. Without doubt there will be setbacks. Your ability to accentuate the positive and bounce back from these will affect your business survival. When you're able to take a situation, reframe it and look at it another way, it's possible to turn the glass from half empty to half full.

Accentuating the positive in any situation and reframing it helps put things into perspective. If something happens that you can't change, at least you can extract something positive from it. Reframing events often creates new opportunities as well. For example, how do you think you would feel if you were the Real Madrid goalkeeper and then suddenly one day you were involved in a car crash and left unable to walk, let alone play football? This happened to Julio Iglesias. Instead of focusing on the hideousness of the situation, he looked for the opportunity and focused on singing, a career that has brought him much success. Reframing allows you to approach situations in an empowering way, as Steph does throughout her story.

Exercise: Reframing

Think of three situations in your life that you tend to dwell on negatively, then think of a positive way to reframe them:

1.
2.
3.

STEP 3: EXPECT A POSITIVE FUTURE

Steph's story is upbeat and full of positive expectations. You may want to read it again and notice the language she uses. There is a high level of expectation that everything will be fine, things will always work out. Here are a few of the positive expectations she has:

- 'I knew I could do it and it was all the employers that assumed I couldn't and I knew they were wrong.'
- 'If you send your brain a message that you can do something then you no doubt can … it will be achieved.'
- 'I believe anything is possible.'

There's a lot of evidence to support the idea that you get what you focus on, so focusing on what you want to achieve and expecting that it will happen is a great strategy. As Steph says, when you tell your brain what you want, suddenly it's more achievable. The reverse is also true. If you focus on what you don't want you'll get more of that. So if you have negative expectations about your future, try putting a more positive spin on them and start filtering for that positive future that you desire. Steph along with many other successful entrepreneurs is living proof that it works.

Exercise: Positive expectations

Write down five negative expectations that you have, then write down the opposite. For example:

1.
2.
3.
4.
5.

Negative future expectation	Positive future expectation
Nothing good ever happens to me	Good things happen to me
I'm too busy to do that	I will find time to do it
No one will want me, I'm not good enough	I am good enough and I will get work

As you finish this chapter, just think for a moment: what are you choosing to filter for the rest of the day? You tend to get what you focus on and you do have a choice over what you filter for. Remember the twins? It's up to you. Are you accentuating the positive, eliminating the negative, or are you messing with Mister In-Between? At the end of the day, it's all about choice – and the choice is yours!

'Most people are about as happy as they make up their minds to be.'
                                                    Abraham Lincoln

Total belief

Believe in what you do.
If you don't,
Then change what you do.

Imagine knowing where you want your business to go, being clearly aware of how you are going to do it and having a product or service that you totally believe in, which you know and have checked is viable. Couple that with an unshakeable belief in yourself and your own abilities and I would say you have a pretty great formula for success!

So where do you start? Always with yourself, then with a robust business plan in whatever format works for you.

Mentoring Moments

I was delivering a training session on how to put together a business plan to a small group of people who were at various stages of setting up their businesses and with very different business ideas. It was as the day progressed that I noticed just how much of a difference it was making to one of the delegates, April Sharpless. It wasn't the content of the course or how I was delivering it that was important, it was the perception that April had of herself and the very different perception others in the room had of her. I have come to know April over the past 12 months and have seen her blossom personally as well as professionally. This is what April shared with me.

Before leaving home that day she had looked in the mirror and the reflection looking back at her was not the person she wanted to be either personally or professionally. April knew that drastic action had to be taken in order to repair her fragile confidence. She had been through a turbulent few months after a tricky divorce and was now a single mother of two young children. April had also left her senior human resources role in an established company to work for herself. She didn't believe in the values and ethics of the company she had left behind and had challenged the board on these issues. She knew there was no going back and that all her bridges were burnt. She felt numb, but knew that it was time to be true to herself and to begin living life according to her own values and ethics. She aimed to feel proud of all her achievements.

April had taken a deep breath and rang three people whom she respected in business: really positive, forward-thinking and down-to-earth people. They were shocked at how lacking in confidence she had become. However, all three showed April a glimmer of hope as they all had the confidence that she could bounce back. She knew that her self-belief was shaky and that all she had for now was theirs, so she would focus on that.

During the business plan course, it became apparent that April was unaware of how the knowledge and abilities that she was sharing with other delegates were respected until another delegate pointed the fact out to her. For April it was a defining moment. What we all saw was an incredibly beautiful woman, inside and out, who was putting her own values into her business plan to do something my own mother taught me: 'always treat others as you would wish to be treated yourself'. At this point April was very close to tears and I quickly realigned the focus back to the practicalities of planning a business.

At the end of the course I had a chat with April and suggested some mentoring for her by a super guy I know, Mike Butterworth. Mike did what I knew he would, he took April under his wing and went through her business planning step by step until she was ready for trading.

Her company, ZEST HR Consultancy, is going from strength to strength and the last time I met April she shared her progress with me. Her ability to become a successful mumpreneur is being fulfilled. I have permission to share this with you in April's own words.

Success

Success is …

- … a sense of engagement, contentment and self-belief
- … looking in the mirror and feeling proud to be me
- … achieved through persistency and honesty
- … being honest with yourself and taking the little knocks as motivators for the bigger challenges in life

Signs of success

Being energized and focused on clear values and morals in your life.

ZEST's mission

Working in partnership with local businesses to add value and ensure compliance, stability and growth.

ZEST's values

ZEST is committed to:

- Exceeding customer requirements
- Quality
- Adding sustainable value
- Continual development
- Knowledge transfer
- Environment

The plans I have

I currently have quite a few strings to my bow and I am unsure which ones will develop into the core offering of ZEST. The first two years of trading will present me with an opportunity to try different things and see what works well and where the demand is.

ZEST's aim

By 1 July 2008, ZEST client base will consist of:

- 1 × management consultancy client
- 2 × HR outsourcing clients – on retainer
- 10 × HR ad hoc clients
- 2 × annual training contracts

The problems I have encountered

- Cost of stationery when I am constantly changing my mind regarding how I want to market myself.
- My lack of IT skills has made me appreciate IT departments more. I no longer have someone on the end of a phone to ask to come and find my document after my PC crashes!
- Sowing seeds and not knowing when the benefits are going to be reaped, if at all.
- Awakening the marketeer in me has been a nightmare. When the risk is as high as it is when you are a sole trader, it is difficult to feel comfortable thinking out of the box. Previously I have always had professional marketeers to do this for me. A good mentor is what is needed.
- Keeping motivated when there is limited direct peer pressure.

My celebrations

- When I eventually set up a back-up system for my PC I sat back with a coffee and felt so much more at ease.
- When my first invoice was paid (three-figure sum), I celebrated with my partner with a glass of wine at home.
- When my second invoice was paid (five-figure sum), I celebrated by making a hair appointment, my first in six months.

Expectations that I have put on myself

- Don't do personal tasks such as paying household bills or signing school consent letters during my working day.

- Elevate and believe in myself as a specialist in my field and develop and maintain appropriate relationships with my clients as a client–consultant as opposed to line manager–employee. The relationship is very different and I have learnt from very early on that I have to take control of this element.

My little goals

- Once I set my working hours out per week, I have to be sure to make the most of the remaining part of the week. My priority is focused around my children and spending quality time with them having *fun* and *laughing* a lot.
- As I have set up ZEST from my home, every Saturday I make conscious arrangements to spend the day out of the house. Too much of the same can be monotonous.
- I diarize to speak to one of my business buddies a week – they are very positive, up-beat people who inspire me to maintain my focus and stay energized.

Have you a plan where you have checked everything you can to ensure your new business is a resounding success? I give out to would-be entrepreneurs the Business Plan Action Chart. Before I do this I take my clients through the visualization that you will find at the end of this chapter. You need to begin with the end in mind, knowing what you actually want.

I would suggest you formulate your plan depending on the way you like to document things and what you will be using the plan for. If you need to borrow money or apply for funding, then a formal plan is necessary. If it is a way of establishing your way forward, then a huge SUCCESS board or an umbrella plan (see Chapter 5) could be for you. Whichever way you choose, use any resources available such as a template from your bank or Business Link.

Remember that if you are competing with others for funds, make your plan attractive! It is a book's cover that usually attracts you to it, you then look at the synopsis before starting to read it in full. Ensure that your business plan does the same and hooks in the recipient by making it stand out from all the rest. When someone picks it up to read, ensure that your summary is as succinct and to the point as possible so your reader's attention is grabbed! This is your golden opportunity. Good luck!

BUSINESS PLAN ACTION CHART

INTRODUCTION	Name; business name; what business does; your vision
SUMMARY	Where business idea came from
	Your character; personality; drive; experience; skills; motivation
	Personal strengths
	Personal background and experience; curriculum vitae
MARKET	Describe your market: niche; fad; seasonal; growing; local; national; international
	Size of market; how you have measured it
	Describe your customers: who; where; how many; demographics

MARKET	Primary research: methods applied; information/results; how you will use this
	Sample questionnaire and/or evidence of primary research
	Secondary research: statistics; trends; surveys/articles; forecasts
	Dangers to your market: how adaptable is your business/product?
BUSINESS AND PERSONAL OBJECTIVES	Make your goals SMART: Specific; Measurable; Achievable/Aspirational; Realistic; Time defined
	Business SWOT: Strengths; Weaknesses; Opportunities; Threats
COMPETITION	Competitor analysis: direct/indirect competition; strengths/weaknesses; unique selling point (USP); who they are; where; what products; what they charge; how they promote
	How you are different from your competitors; what is your USP?
	Features and benefits of your product
MARKETING ACTIVITY	How will your customers know you exist; where will they find you?
	Business and product/service image: logo; brand; image; first impression
	How will customers easily identify your USP?
	What daily, weekly, monthly promotions are in place? Evidence of a marketing plan: method, dates, costs, goals. Show how this relates to your sales assumptions and cash-flow forecast

(Continued)

HOW YOUR BUSINESS WILL RUN	Premises: research on lease, rent, rates, legal issues, etc.
	Staff; employment law
	Working from home: reasons for; overcoming issues; planning consent; neighbours
	Sole trader; partnership; limited company; insurance; legal issues
	Licences; health and safety; terms of trade; Disability Discrimination Act; professional advice
	VAT registration; Inland Revenue registration
	Patents; copyright; intellectual property, trade marks; business name registration
FINANCIALS	**PERSONAL SURVIVAL BUDGET**
	Costings: variable; fixed
	Selling price: how did you arrive at your price; what did you consider?
	Identify start-up costs
	Cash-flow forecast
	Cash-flow assumptions
	Break-even analysis: what sales revenue is needed; units to sell; what price per unit
	Projected profit or loss
	'What if' analysis: assessing the risks; what could happen; what the effect is on your business; preventive steps

Entrepreneur's Experience

I had begun my training business with very little planning. I was returning to work after having children and knew that I wanted the hours I
worked to fit around the school day. I wrote a list of what training I could
deliver and what I believed companies needed and would pay for, then
I simply picked up the phone to a few contacts I had and began touting
for business. I managed to secure a few appointments that in turn led to
contracts and away I went. Great, I thought, I have my own business!

A few months down the line I realized I was still in the same position –
quoting and delivering any kind of training that anyone wanted. I had
no clarity and direction. I didn't know where I was going. I had no idea
what I specialized in or what my marketplace was.

It was pointed out to me that planning a business was the same as
planning to travel. When you go on a car journey you need to know
the following, most basic of things:

• Where are you going?
• What route are you going to take?
• What are the contingencies if there are diversions?

If these plans aren't in place it is impossible to arrive at your destination. This seems obvious now. I spent some time planning my business
and my personal life around it, realizing that I had one life and all I did
in it had to fit!

I now have a plan and I have it displayed on my office wall at home.
It makes me feel much more focused and comfortable, as I finally know
where I am going. I pick and choose the profitable training that I special-
ize in and love doing and it fits around the children's term times too!

Making It – Meeting Josephine LaVey,
LaVey Corsetry & Clothing

'Every day I walk into my workshop, look around, smile and feel so proud.' For Josephine LaVey it is a dream that she has now realized, but one that has taken her on a roller-coaster ride of believing in herself.

Josephine explains, 'I design and manufacture unique corsetry and clothing that caters for all sizes. My clothes are not for the faint hearted, but once you're laced in there will be no looking back. My clothes bring a feeling of power and femininity.'

Josephine's journey has taken her from being a wild 15 year old courting with trouble, to becoming a successful businesswoman creating and selling her products around the world. She has achieved a first class honours degree, a master's from a top American University, a presentation from Prince Charles and an enormous sense of pride.

Josephine's face jumped out at me from the pages of the *Leicester Mercury*. She was holding a Union Jack corset and the article began with the word **SUCCESS**. I picked up the phone and arranged to meet her.

A size 26, Josephine has always made her own clothes, which is how she became inspired to create her company, LaVey Corsetry & Clothing.

When I met her she was dressed in full gothic style. 'I wear my own designs,' she said. 'I used to get lots of interest. I used to have bigger girls approach me and ask me where I got my outfits from. So one day I held a stall at the Whitby Gothic Festival – I'd sold out by 2 P.M. I really enjoyed it and was ready to put the wheels in motion to start my own business.'

Josephine's workshop is one of many housed in a drab building in an undesirable part of town. As I walked through the door the stunning clothes that filled the space immediately distracted me. They were mainly corsets used for outerwear in an assortment of colours made from rich fabrics, they seemed to be hanging everywhere and it reminded me of a theatre dressing room during a show. Quite clearly, Josephine's work fits the 'creative industry' title beautifully. I was intrigued about how it all happened and how Josephine's business came to be.

'It was really weird,' Josephine explained, 'because when I was nominated for The Prince's Trust business of the year award and invited to the palace, I didn't really know what to think … I was like, "Oh, all right then." I was introduced to The Prince's Trust through my college. I went to an open evening, which Business Link attended too; they were really helpful with stuff like a business plan. I did the business plan first, got a bank account and then applied for funding to The Prince's Trust. The Trust also puts you in touch with a business mentor, although I was left in limbo for about a year because there wasn't anyone in the Leicester office that could help my kind of business. During the year I was just plodding, doing my work out of my spare bedroom – it was more like a hobby.

'The change came for me when locally there was a push on creative industries. As I came under that umbrella I was given mentoring help from a guy in London. He had some experience helping businesses in the sex wear market. I was really unsure of myself and he kept pushing me and helping me to believe that I could do it. He was a real inspiration to me. There was one part of my head that kept telling me that I might fail and that I wasn't good enough to succeed. He was the person who kept me positive and said things like, "I don't think you know how impressed people are by you." Soon the other side of my head started to say to me, "I'm going for it". I began to realize that it's not about being boastful, it's about being proud of what you are achieving. I also realized that for every successful person there will always be ten people questioning, "Who do they think they are?" I decided to "go for it" and enjoy the support I was given.

'I asked for a loan of £1500 from The Prince's Trust, which they gave to me; they also gave me a grant of £500. I already had my own sewing machine and I knew I wanted to keep costs to the minimum. It was such a huge help to getting me started and I will always feel grateful to them. Each year, young people who are being helped by the Trust are entered for the annual awards. First I won the East Midlands award; I still didn't really think that it was any big deal. But then when you go and meet Prince Charles at the palace, I thought "Oh my God, me at the palace!" Other people were really jealous about it and I thought, "Well, don't get too big for your boots, Josephine." I was really excited and although I didn't win one of the awards, they had said right at the beginning before they started to announce the winners that they were doing something that had never been done before and had made a special award for somebody. It was a highly commended award and I was the winner! I was more pleased about winning that than the first prize, because they had made something special just for me.

'In the beginning I had just been pottering around in my spare bedroom as I was holding on to my dream of doing more work with the theatre. My dream was to make costumes for the array of shows that are put on at Leicester's Haymarket Theatre and create magical costumes.'

Josephine took out the most beautiful sketch of a dress destined for a ballet company that I have ever seen, the intricate detail and thought that had gone into it was amazing. Her dream was sadly not to be fulfilled, as the senior wardrobe mistress didn't stick to her word and it seemed the more costume designing and making work that was promised to Josephine, the more the staff there relished in not giving it to her. As more things happened and she became more heartbroken, Josephine knew she had to walk away, as it was clear that her face didn't fit and her career at the Haymarket wasn't going anywhere. I wondered if Josephine felt content with the path she was on right now and was happy for her initial dream to remain on hold.

'Yes, I am,' she said. 'I don't know if you would call it fate because I'm at the beginning of it all right now, but I have in a way glimpses into the future. I was sitting on a bus one day and kind of disappeared: I saw myself in a big office somewhere talking to lots of people, saying what I wanted doing, I was in my 50s and really successful. That's why I am enjoying doing what I'm doing now at this early stage, because I know that one day I will look back to the old days when I couldn't afford to pay the gas bill and all that sort of thing. So now even when I am struggling I am trying to enjoy it, so when I am that 50 year old with the big company I don't get complacent.

'I want to run my own business, but as well I am really keen on helping other people. I have had another dream about an old cinema in Leicester, down Rutland Street. I dreamt about buying it and turning it into lots of little workspaces and little shops for new businesses, artists and designers that can't afford much. So they can come straight from college and get started.

'I do think that sometimes my work and wanting to help other creative people kind of replaces the childlessness in my life, knowing that I am nurturing people in another way. I have made the decision not to have any children, so my business and helping other businesses are my babies.

'Ever since I was a kid, I was always the big dreamer but I didn't believe in myself, I always thought that I would never amount to much more than working at Tesco. I left home at 15 and got into trouble and stuff, I went a bit wild and got into drugs and alcohol, which of course I am not proud of now. Even then I was always the one who would make all the big plans thinking it would never happen. I didn't feel that anyone believed in me. My mum once told me that a certain member of my family was really shocked when I graduated as they always thought I would be a nobody. In fact, I can imagine those cosy chats around cups of coffee with them all calling me that.

'At 24 I made up my mind to do something about my dreams and took a costume course at De Montfort University. That progressed to a first class honours degree. I then won two scholarships for universities in America, one in Illinois, Chicago and one in Indiana. I heard about the scholarships through my university, they were incredibly helpful to me. The day I walked out of there with my graduate's piece of paper I suddenly thought, "Oh my God, I can do something!" You know what I mean, I wasn't a waste of space any more and I'm not a failure.

'I have not only got a degree but a first class degree and I'm dyslexic as well, against all those odds, and I paid my own way through my education. I had three jobs, I used to go straight from college and iron all night at this place doing people's laundry and all sorts of things, they were really heavy horrible jobs, but it was worth it. I had my paper and I was going to America – 800 people from all over the world applied for the place and it was me who was chosen. When my tutor came in and said "Jo, not only have you got Illinois you've also got Indiana, they both want to offer you a place!" I couldn't take it in, everybody in class was looking at me, they were all smiling and clapping, so pleased for me. I just burst into tears, I was in shock, all I could think was, "How am I going to get all my shoes there?" It was hard to take in. I was being paid to go halfway across the world. It felt really good.

'Going to America was a huge change for me, because I was going to a place where nobody knew my past or me. They had no preconceptions about me. I decided I wanted people to treat me with respect. I didn't have any of the baggage I had in Leicester with people knowing me when I was young. I walked in with a really confident attitude, so people took me as they found me and treated me with the respect that I knew I deserved. I had gone through a huge transformation and I was no longer the person I used to be. When I came home a lot of people found it really hard not to be jealous, although my close friends were very pleased and proud for me. One old friend refused to see me, but that's her stuff.

'It was on my return that I began making clothes and trying to sell them. I began with people that I knew and that spread through word of mouth. The first time I had to go out to get some business was hard. I took some corsets into a shop in Leicester to ask if the owner would stock them – I got a "no". The second shop I went into I got a "yes", however – she ended up wearing them herself!

'It was actually by chance that I began retailing my products. I was in Blink in Burlingtons Arcade, Leicester. A customer came in and asked at the counter if they sold corsets. I was there at the counter with my friend and she said, "Jo makes them." The owners of Blink asked me to bring some in and it went from there. Blink have been great, they showed me how other people do their business orders, where the trade fairs were and have helped with loads of advice. I am now making gothic clothes for other shops, this is a marketplace I know well and feel confident in. I am also going to do another trade show in London called Pure Woman, which is women's wear. After recent success at a trade fair I am now exporting to Germany and Helsinki too.'

Josephine gets her inspiration from Vivienne Westwood, who she feels is one of the great names in British fashion. Westwood is called the 'lady of punk fashion' – Josephine would love to be known as the 'dark lady of fashion'. While reading a book about Vivienne Westwood it struck Josephine that she was such a 'normal' person, that recognition hadn't altered her in any way. She talked about when she used to have to do moonlight flits from one shop to another or from where she lived, as she couldn't afford to pay the rent. Josephine aspires to be like that when she is older and more successful.

'I keep thinking that I must remember what it is like now so when I am asked for advice from somebody young in the future, I can still relate to them. You are not going to appreciate that million-pound house or anything if you don't remember what it's like now. I went through a religious stage when I was 20, I wanted to become a nun, and I burnt all my possessions – my clothes, my records and stuff. It was a really liberating experience as it was just stuff. I now know that if my unit burnt down tomorrow even though I had spent so long making it the way it is, that having nothing can't take away from what I have inside. I have the resilience to say "Right, where can I get a secondhand sewing machine from?" and start all over again.'

Looking around me I can see that Josephine is the mistress of innovative designs and ideas. She tells me that she can already see the future marketing campaigns in her head. When she is creating design shows and so on she always sees the show very clearly first.

'I can sit and watch it like I'm in the audience. It's the same with my collection; I can see the whole thing right down to the tiniest detail. I'm a very visual person. When I create something it's like when I watch people play the piano and they go off into another world, I do that when I'm making clothes. When it's finished, if it's something I am particularly proud of I look at it for hours and feel really pleased. Maybe it's a bit vain, but I want to leave something behind when I'm no longer on this earth that people remember me for, I want to leave a footprint behind, make my mark. I want to do it in a big way too.'

Josephine finds sustaining her enthusiasm for her work easy because she has such a passion for it. 'I love it, I always look forward to coming in to my workshop and making the next corset. I am here 13 hours a day sometimes; I do just lose myself in what I am doing. I feel very privileged. Also, because I am building my confidence slowly from my own little empire, I know that both will grow and grow. My vision is that there will be a whole team of people just striving for one thing, to be a fabulous team and to make fabulous clothes. I like the idea of everyone contributing with their ideas and everyone progressing and being fulfilled in what they do. I love it when I go to the gothic festivals and there are lots of people walking around in my clothes. That's how I see it, I will be able to go up to them and say, "Oh, you are wearing one of my outfits and you look fab."'

I asked Josephine what advice she would give to someone about to begin their own enterprise. 'If you want it bad enough you will find a way to make it happen,' she said. 'You just have to be pig headed, put the blinkers on and really go for what you want to do. There are plenty of places that will give you lots of help. Look at yourself and see if you are 100 per cent dedicated to that dream and whether you are going to do it. Be completely honest with yourself, because it will be a lot of hard work. Look into the mirror often and say "I'm fabulous" and although it can be an uphill struggle, make the journey in fabulous shoes!'

Since I interviewed Josephine her business has continued to go from strength to strength. Now her creations are sold in more than 40 wholesalers in seven different countries, as well as from her shop in Loseby Lane, Leicester, an exclusive shopping area. Her pieces have been featured in films – including the cult vampire flick *Underworld* – and in photo shoots for the multimillion-selling Goth metal band Cradle of Filth. Josephine delights in supporting The Prince's Trust herself in Leicester and is true to her word by 'putting something back'.

Interestingly, there is a cultural quarter being developed in the area of Leicester where Josephine predicted, including a new multi-million-pound theatre. Parts of this development are 'creative industry' business incubation units, where Josephine's inspiration is prominent.

The following are extracts from a speech made by His Royal Highness The Prince of Wales, talking about the young people The Prince's Trust has helped (reproduced with the kind permission of HRH The Prince of Wales).

'My admiration for all that they have achieved is boundless and I cannot begin to tell you how proud I am of each and every one of them.

'They have all had to overcome some extraordinary hurdles to achieve success, and it just proves what can be accomplished if we can only give young people the right support at the right time. Of course, not everyone is suited to running their own business, but there are a great many young people out there with real talent and a good idea who only lack belief in themselves, and the necessary financial support, to start them on their way.

'All I ever wanted to do with my Trust was to make an investment in the future so that young people could realize their full potential for themselves, for their communities and for the nation. I think you can perhaps now understand why I feel so proud of all those we have helped and why I take such a personal interest in them.

'The young people we have helped have overcome obstacles which would have defeated most of us: long-term unemployment, ill-health, injury, lack of education and qualifications, drug dependency, time spent in prison, poverty and a lack of faith in them as people. The banks and other funding bodies turned them away as too high a risk, but The Prince's Trust refused to judge them by their past and their background and, instead, saw their potential.'

Making It Happen for You – Total Belief

What did Josephine do?

- Recognized that her lack of self-belief limited her potential.
- Decided to use more empowering self-beliefs.
- Put her old limiting beliefs where they belonged – in the past.
- Found new and empowering beliefs about herself.
- Totally believed in the new beliefs and *success*.

How can you model Josephine and have total belief in yourself?

- Identify the beliefs that limit you.
- Make a decision to change those beliefs.
- Put your old beliefs in the past.
- Choose some new empowering beliefs.
- Take on the new beliefs and just wait for success to come knocking on your door.

Do you really believe in yourself?

Think about what you really want to achieve in your business. With that in mind, score yourself from 0 to 10 on the statements below. A score of 0 means you really disagree and a score of 10 means you really agree.

- I believe it is totally possible to achieve my dream.
- I have a great desire to achieve my dream.
- I often imagine myself achieving my dream.
- I deserve to achieve my dream.
- When I have doubts about my dream, I am still able to carry on.
- I am able to put other people's criticisms to one side.
- It's my own responsibility to achieve my dream.
- My life will be better when I achieve my dream.
- I can achieve my dream without losing my identity.
- I am surrounded by people who believe in me.

CHECK YOUR ATTITUDE

Add up the total score out of 100.

- *If you scored 85–100 points* – You have a strong belief in yourself. Use the exercises below to identify any chinks in the armour of your self-belief. See if you can get your score even higher.
- *If you scored 50–84 points* – You have an element of self-doubt creeping in that needs to be worked on.
- *If you scored 0–49 points* – You probably have a lot of doubt and must build your self-belief if you really want to move forward with your dreams.

Five Steps to Achieve Total Belief in Yourself

We all have doubts, don't we? Does my bum look big in this? Do they like me? Can I really do this? It's normal to have doubts, and sometimes it's helpful. If you're about to jump out of a plane with no parachute, a little self-doubt comes in very handy.

Unfortunately, our beliefs sometimes limit us in an unhelpful way. They prevent us from achieving things that with total belief in ourselves we could easily do. Often lack of belief is an attempt to protect us from something. In the case of the plane jump with no parachute it's obvious. In the case of a business start-up, it's not always so clear what our doubts are shielding us from, but often it's the fear of failure – or even the fear of success. What might happen if we succeeded? Would life still be the same? Would our friends still like us? Would we change beyond all recognition? Crazy as it sounds, we often try to protect the status quo, because we are fearful of the change that success might bring or indeed the disappointment and humiliation of failure. If we don't try then failure isn't an option, so we hold back and doubt ourselves.

Just as believing in yourself will move you forward, limiting beliefs and self-doubt have a really nasty habit of keeping you exactly where you are and preventing you from making progress. For example, the belief 'I'm not credible' could be protecting you from looking foolish if you fail. It has a positive intent for you, but believing it is a sure fire way of keeping you right where you are now. It's like a ball and chain, sabotaging your efforts to succeed. Limiting beliefs are the fuel for the fire of your self-doubt. If you want a limitless future, you absolutely have to tame your self-doubt and allow space in your mind for the part of you that totally believes in your ability to succeed.

If we take Josephine as an example, we see that she had limiting beliefs in the beginning. One of them was: 'I was always the big dreamer but I didn't believe in myself. I always thought that I would never amount to much more than working at Tesco.' If she'd hung on to that belief for too long, I think we can all hazard a fairly good guess at what she might be doing now. Good for her, she got rid of it. Not that there's anything wrong with working at Tesco, but it didn't serve her higher goal of achieving her dreams.

If you want to stamp out self-doubt, you need to identify your limiting beliefs. What are your demons of doubt? What do you believe about yourself right now that's holding you back? Get them down on paper so you can deal with them.

STEP 1: WRITE DOWN THE BELIEFS THAT LIMIT YOU

Take a look at the examples of self-doubting, limiting beliefs in the box. Then write down all your own self-doubting beliefs. As you do notice how you feel and ask yourself the question: 'Do these beliefs serve me well?'

Self-doubting limiting belief	Purpose of the belief	Does it belong in the past/ can I make it empowering?	New empowering belief
I can't set up a business because I'm just not creative enough	If I don't bother to set up my business, I cannot fail. Nothing ventured, nothing lost	Yes	I don't know how to set up a business yet. I am creative enough to set up a fabulous business. Nothing ventured nothing gained
I'm not credible	Saves me from looking stupid	Yes	I am very credible and people respect me

Self-doubting limiting belief	Purpose of the belief	Does it belong in the past/ can I make it empowering?	New empowering belief
Who would listen to me, nobody would take me seriously	Saves me from embarrassing myself	Yes	How do I get people to listen to me? I have got something great to offer the world

STEP 2: DECIDE WHICH OF THE LIMITING BELIEFS YOU DON'T NEED

Writing down your self-doubting beliefs is one thing. Getting rid of them is quite another. Deciding which ones you don't need any more is as difficult as trying to weed through a wardrobe full of old clothes. You know you should cull your collection, but even though much of it is totally out of fashion, not very flattering and you've not worn it for years, you insist on hanging on to it all. Every time you open the wardrobe, staring back at you, among many other similar garments, is a green jacket with large blue buttons and huge shoulder pads that you haven't worn since 1993. It gets in the way of all the other clothes you could be wearing, if only you could see them.

We do the same with our beliefs: we keep them when we don't need them any more. Some of them have been with us for years. Despite the fact they're unflattering, like a pair of old leggings, we find them comfortable and familiar and insist on keeping them. Heaven forbid, we occasionally wear them. It's worth acknowledging that limiting beliefs sometimes hold us back as a form of protection against success, but if you want success you've got to get rid of these beliefs. Make room for something new. If they won't go, change them so that they work for you more positively.

Early on in her story, Josephine had limiting beliefs that caused her to doubt herself, but she made a decision not to take any notice of them as they didn't serve her goal. She decided to listen to the voice in her head that was telling her 'Go for it' rather than the one that told her 'You might fail and you're not good enough to succeed'. She decided to do something about her dreams, so she kicked out her voice of doubt and got on with it.

Exercise: Limiting beliefs

Look at the limiting beliefs you wrote down. Which ones are stopping you from moving forward and robbing you of your self-belief?

As you look, acknowledge that these beliefs are trying to help you in some way. Are your beliefs an attempt to prevent you from failing, looking stupid or just making sure you don't overload yourself? It could be anything.

Decide what the purpose of your limiting belief could be and write it down in the box. Ask yourself: 'Do I need this belief?' 'Does this belief belong in the past?' 'Can I make it more empowering?' Write 'yes' or 'no' in the next box. If you've got at least one 'yes', you're ready for Step 3.

STEP 3: PUT YOUR OLD BELIEFS IN THE PAST

When Josephine arrived in America, she'd left all her baggage in Leicester and I don't think she meant her shoes! She was talking about her limiting beliefs. You too can put your disempowering beliefs where they belong. It would be a little unfair to send everybody's to Leicester, so I'm going to suggest somewhere else. Based on an exercise developed by Robert Dilts (2000), try the following to put your disempowering beliefs back where they belong, in the past.

Exercise: Put your beliefs in the past

Imagine for a moment that you are standing in your own personal museum. In this museum you can put anything from your life that you no longer need, safe in the knowledge that you can always visit it if you need to. In this museum there's a whole section for beliefs that you just don't need any more. Your beliefs in Father Christmas and the Tooth Fairy are there, as well as your belief that Duran Duran were the centre of the universe and that the small, spotty boy at the school disco was your true love. All manner of beliefs are there that were valuable at some point in your past, but are no longer relevant or helpful. Just as technology moves on and causes things to date, so has your life, and some of your beliefs are outdated.

Imagine that you can literally take your old disempowering beliefs and put them into your museum, along with all the others you don't need.

One at a time, as you put each of your old beliefs carefully into the museum, just think about what form they take. Are they pictures, statues, artefacts, maybe even a dinosaur? Take a moment in your mind's eye to look at your old beliefs in the museum. As you look ask yourself: 'What is the consequence of holding on to these beliefs and not leaving them in the museum?' Think about what your future will be like with your old beliefs where they belong. Notice how this looks, feels and sounds.

STEP 4: CHOOSE SOME NEW BELIEFS

Just as deciding to get rid of old beliefs can be like culling your wardrobe, taking on fresh ones can be like restocking it with fabulous new clothes. Let's face it, who doesn't like shopping for new clothes? Well, you have permission. You can now shop till you drop, even if it's only in your mind. Think about this as a no-holds-barred shopping expedition to the clothes store of your dreams. Helpful assistants allow you to try on anything you like. When you've purchased all you desire, it's wrapped up in gold tissue paper and popped into glossy bags for you to take home. We're talking Prada, we're talking Gucci and we're talking LaVey! Anything you want. Guess what, even your old clothes, that green jacket, can be restyled, so if you still really want it, it can be updated so it suits the 'you' of today not the 'you' of 1993. So here we go, fill your boxes and bags with new empowering beliefs about yourself – beliefs that will serve you well and really suit you.

Let's take a look at what Josephine did to turn around or leave behind some of her self-doubting, limiting beliefs. One of her beliefs was that she was 'a waste of space'. She turned this into a new, empowering belief, 'I can do something'. She updated it, restyled it and left the old one behind.

Sometimes just a slight change in the way you talk about your beliefs can make all the difference. Instead of saying 'I don't know how to market my business', try this on for size: 'I don't know how to market my business *yet*.'

State your new beliefs positively, so that they reflect things you are rather than things that you aren't. For example, if you are 'not a failure', what are you? You are 'a success'. If you are 'not a waste of space', what are you? You are 'a useful person people want to have around'.

EXERCISE: EMPOWERING BELIEFS

List	1	2	3	4	5

Write your new, empowering beliefs from Step 1 in the table above. As you do, say them out loud. Cross out the old ones. Now ask yourself these questions:

- 'What is the logical consequence of believing my new beliefs?'
- 'What would it be like if I believed this totally and absolutely with all my being and lived my life as if it were true?'

STEP 5: TAKE ON THE NEW BELIEFS AND LOOK OUT FOR SUCCESS TO COME KNOCKING ON YOUR DOOR!

Ever heard the phrase 'When I see it, I'll believe it?' Help to embrace and wear your new beliefs by seeing them in action. If you can imagine yourself living as if all your new beliefs are true, it will make them more likely to stick.

Top athletes use visualization, the technique of seeing their future successes, to help them in sports training. They imagine themselves winning races they've never run. They prepare mentally and physically to win. Winning a race isn't always a surprise to them, because in their minds they've won a thousand times before. Josephine uses this technique of visualizing when she sees quite clearly in her mind's eye the success she'll be enjoying in her 50s: 'I saw myself in a big office somewhere talking to lots of people, saying what I wanted doing. I was in my 50s and really successful.'

Exercise: Visualization

Experience your future success by trying this visualization.

Sit in a comfortable chair. From this chair you are going to become the director of a new blockbusting movie, called *My Success*. In front of you is a large screen where you, as director, are going to preview this fabulous new film. You have total artistic and creative control. It's a story about you. It charts the success you achieved after you got total belief in yourself.

When you're ready for the action to begin, in your mind's eye see the successful you on the screen. Notice how you are. Who else is there? Is there any sound? How do you feel? Make the picture clear, make it large and make it in colour. Make the sounds clear. Make it a moving film. Really play around with it: as director you can do whatever you like. Do you want to play the really good bits in slow motion? Bring it closer, move it further away, keep editing until this really is fabulous and you feel fantastic watching it.

Then imagine that you are in the film. You're not just watching yourself from the chair, you're really in it, experiencing everything that the 'you' on the screen is experiencing, hearing what she's hearing and seeing what she's seeing. Enjoy this movie and only when you're ready come back to the director's seat.

Do this every day as many times as you like. Have fun with the images. Do the visualization in the bath, on the bus, when you're bored. Do it whenever you can. You are training your brain to expect and anticipate success.

As you begin to get total belief in yourself, make sure that you surround yourself with others who have the same belief in your abilities as you do. Combined with your heightened level of self-belief, doing this will propel you forward in a way you could probably never have imagined before.

Perhaps you'd prefer to take some advice from someone who changed the landscape of popular entertainment. This person certainly knew a thing or two about success and the crucial part that total self-belief plays in achieving it.

'Somehow I can't believe that there are any heights that can't be scaled by a man who knows the secrets of making dreams come true. This special secret, it seems to me, can be summarized in four Cs. They are curiosity, courage, and constancy, and the greatest of all is confidence. When you believe in a thing, believe in it all the way, implicitly and unquestionably.'

Walt Disney

Trust

Be open and honest,
remember that your behaviour is mirrored
back to you

Trust for me is paramount in any relationship, business or otherwise. There have been a few business situations that I and others have been in where the trust has been broken. Personally, I don't go back there. If you continue to do business with someone when the trust has been broken, how can you be sure of the outcome? I also aim to be open and honest when doing business myself. I don't want to be in a position of having to look over my shoulder waiting to be found out. Therefore, I hold my hand up to my mistakes and apologize and in turn enjoy celebrating my successes. I accept that I am human and doing the best I can.

I also believe that using your instincts is an integral part of trust. Later in the book you will read the story of Lynne Franks and the SEED Women's Enterprise Programme. When I first did business with Lynne the programme was being created and was the first of its kind. We didn't know where it was going, so how could we set firm guidelines? We couldn't – what we did do is have a working relationship based on trust. I am delighted to say that it worked very well. We both used our instincts and it felt right. If it feels right it usually is.

When I gave birth to my third daughter I had been in labour for many hours, tests had been done and there were no medical signs of the baby being in distress. However, the registrar (who had shared with me that it was his first day) had a very strong instinct that something was wrong. So had I. He asked if I was willing to sign a consent form for a caesarean based on gut instinct. As I was feeling the same and I trusted him, I agreed. I knew that other professionals present disagreed and that if I ignored my instincts I would live to regret it. I insisted on staying awake while my baby was born and had an epidural caesarean. As soon as Martha was delivered, the operating theatre went very quiet. No-one was sure if she was alive. Again, I had a strong instinct that she would be fine. Fortunately, Martha was resuscitated and is now a healthy 10 year old. I had asked not to be made aware of what was going on during delivery as it was all I could handle being operated on whilst awake. I did ask to have the birth explained to me afterwards. When I was visited for this discussion the following day, I learnt that if it weren't for the registrar using his instincts we would have lost her. Martha had minutes left to live. From that day onwards I have learnt to trust my instincts in all areas of my life.

Mentoring Moments

I was one of the trainers on a nationwide funded programme called the New Entrepreneur Scholarship. It entailed a 12-week business training course addressing emotional and practical needs, as well as weekly one-to-one advisory sessions. If after 12 weeks the delegates had produced a viable business plan, they were entitled to funding towards business start-up costs.

For me it was a pleasure to be part of such a programme because I was able to see the delegates blossom and grow in confidence and to see their businesses succeed too. One particular guy had a real trust issue to overcome. He had just come out of prison and he was at the lowest point in his life. He trusted no one, particularly the people who had said they would help him. He also didn't trust himself. During the 12 weeks we were with him he shared with our group of delegates that he was gradually learning to trust us. He began to feel worthy again, he knew we believed in him when people in other areas of his life didn't. I felt more confident that we could get somewhere with him. Recently, I saw him at a networking event, suited, booted and laughing that he had done it. I am so proud of him, as learning to trust again has brought him so much success.

When you are recruiting the services of a business professional such as a mentor, adviser or accountant, ensure that you gel with the person, even if their service is free. You will both get so much more out of the relationship if it 'feels right'.

Entrepreneur's Experience

As a freelance dance teacher, I was asked to choreograph a modern jazz championship dance for an 11-year-old pupil who by any standards was exceptional. I worked with her for some time, establishing her strengths and making sure that her two minutes of solo dance exploited them. I realized I was pushing her to her limits and challenged myself on more than one occasion if I was pushing the boundaries too far. We worked together for a number of weeks building up to the championship performance.

I remember sitting in the audience wanting to be sick, I was so scared. I had given her some very complicated steps to perform. She was a beautiful 'leggy' dancer and I had begun her routine with (I will aim to describe this in non-technical terms!) a balance on one leg, taking her working leg up to her ear at the front and rotating it to her side and then behind her very slowly, keeping it very high. When her leg was behind her she then leant her body towards the floor with her nose on her knee, taking her leg into an 'arabesque' behind her, as high as her leg could go. As it sounds, this is a hard balance for a dance professional to accomplish and here was I giving it to an 11 year old.

I knew I was taking a risk, a huge risk. I knew that if the first section was performed as well as she could she would probably win the championship. If she blew it, she didn't stand a chance. I was asking her to do this publicly. Her parents were blissfully unaware just how talented their daughter was and the level of risk I was taking with her.

She entered the stage and was amazing. She won the championship and later that year was accepted into White Lodge full time, the junior department of the Royal Ballet School.

I asked the owner of the dance school why she had asked me to choreograph the dance and she replied, 'I trusted you to take the risk and prove to her and her parents how good she really is.' How glad I am that it worked.

Making it – Meeting Sarah Pharo, Pharo Communications

Pharo Communications was founded by Sarah Pharo and specializes in PR and marketing for the agricultural sector. Sarah has more than 20 years' experience in devising, creating and running media campaigns all over the world and boasts clients such as Nestlé, Bayer and Pink Lady apples. Formerly a journalist with local and national publications in the UK, Sarah saw a gap in the market place and filled it.

I was invited into Pharo Communications by Business Link Coventry together with Dee, my then 'partner in crime' and the best IT trainer I have ever come across. Business Link had asked us to conduct a training needs analysis for the company, which was in a period of consolidation and getting ready to upskill the workforce and drive the company forwards into new areas. At the time I was delivering the Small and Medium Enterprise Work-Skills Project for Business Link. Dee and I were responsible for getting organizations in Warwickshire rocking and rolling and understanding their computer systems like never before.

We arrived at Stoneleigh Agricultural Park on a bright spring morning and it struck me as we pulled through the main entrance what a fabulous place it was to house agricultural companies. The companies and exhibition centre are set all around the main arena and beyond. Stoneleigh is owned by the Royal Agricultural Society of England and is home to the Royal Show.

When we met Sarah we quickly realized we were dealing with an astute businesswoman with a creative flair who knew her stuff and didn't suffer fools gladly. I knew that to gain rapport with her I needed to respond in the same authoritative manner she used and ensure that she understood our credibility. Doing our homework on the company before we met certainly went in our favour and Sarah put her trust in us to help her company.

The day was about the questions 'Where are we now? Where do we want to go? And how are we going to get there?' Pharo was having a 'reality check', as I like to call it, and was also updating its computer systems to cope with the expansion ahead. Sarah invited staff in one by one to talk to us, in her presence, and encouraged their honest opinions on their own and the company's strengths and weaknesses, the opportunities they saw and the threats they and the company might encounter. I have never experienced such openness before: usually embarrassment surrounds problems and mistakes, with blame firmly laid at someone else's door. Here with Sarah and her team, the mistakes were viewed as learning curves and the problems as opportunities. If people needed help to improve then Sarah was willing to support them.

We spent the morning conducting individual interviews, where the presiding factors to explore were mutual respect, openness, honesty and trust. The morning session cumulated in a group discussion with everyone taking part. A beautiful lunch by outside caterers was brought in and what we thought was a large stationery cupboard turned out to be a wine store and bottles of red and white were opened and shared. This is definitely the way to treat people and it was evident that a valued workforce all coming together for the mutual good of the company was commonplace.

Usually there is an element of 'cloak and dagger' even when people in a company are overtly being open and honest with each other, particularly through a period of change or growth. This almost always leads to a breakdown in communication and a 'them and us' attitude developing between the management team and the workforce. For any company to function at the highest level there needs to be a foundation of excellent communication. Sarah had found the key: she gave people responsibility for their work and their clients, ensuring that there was a communications platform for all, and it worked. I was intrigued to discover more about her as a person and Pharo Communications' journey.

Sarah was brought up on the Isle of Wight and went to college in Portsmouth to participate in the National Council for the Training of Journalists Course, after which she went to work for a local paper as a journalist. On the advice of a friend she then went to work for *Farmers' Weekly*.

'I had absolutely no technical knowledge on farming whatsoever,' she said, 'and I realize I was very lucky as they were looking for journalists they could teach about farming rather than agriculturalists who could write. I was interviewed by probably the five most influential men in agriculture at the time and I was a complete wreck. I was so nervous as *Farmers' Weekly* was the top journal of its day and probably still is. It was also published in the hub of British journalism, Fleet Street. I went along feeling that I didn't stand a chance and halfway through the interview it hit me that this sounded a really interesting job. I left the interview with them asking me to go away, get a local story, write it up and send it to them. I found a story about a local sheep farmer, sent it to them and to my amazement got the job! I then spent a very happy five years there and only left when I became pregnant.

'I had every intention of being a full-time mum and housewife and maybe go back to work in my latter years. After Emma was born I felt very differently. I loved Emma and loved being with her, but I felt that the challenge in my life had gone. I found myself having conversations about how many teeth the baby has and how many nappies I got through a day. My husband was working in London at the Ministry of Defence and to be fair I think he found it frustrating too, as instead of having a good challenging discussion when he got home, all I could talk about was mumsy stuff. I managed like this for about six months and tried to accept the change, but after that I felt like I wanted to throw everything out of the window. I have a lot of sympathy for new mothers who find it hard to cope with the change that being a stay-at-home parent brings as it is a radical change, particularly after being in an interesting, busy business. My life used to consist of going to press conferences, travelling a lot, staying away in hotels, meeting interesting people, I was involved in politics, I would be at dinner with all the heads of industry. Suddenly that had all disappeared from my life and it wasn't the same reading about it in a magazine.

'One of the good things about a career in journalism is being able to freelance. There was a young girl of 18 who lived next door but one to me who wanted to be a children's nanny, so she used to come and look after Emma for the odd days when I was out working. I also did quite a bit of work from home and this proved very successful. I had my second daughter Sam and got back into freelancing a lot sooner, which worked well. *Farming News*, a new paper set up to rival *Farmers' Weekly*, offered me a job. I decided this was a good opportunity for me and knew it was time to formalize my childcare arrangements. My part-time nanny took full charge of the children and I believe that was a crucial decision on my behalf, as I felt that I couldn't do a job half-heartedly. If I'm honest, at the time I did feel guilty for leaving the children, but only because others' perception of the situation made me feel guilty. I love my children dearly, but I didn't feel stimulated by them when they were babies, I'm not a naturally maternal mother. Going back to work gave me the challenge and level of intellectual conversation that I missed. I realize I was in the minority, as it was about 28 years ago and attitudes to working mothers were very different then.

'I worked there for another two years before realizing that I had gone as far as I could in journalism. I was constantly taking enquiries from people asking me why I hadn't chosen to run a story and what was it about the ones I had chosen that worked. I think there was a lot of misconception from companies about how to write press releases. What was a story? How do you interest a reader? It was then that I realized there was a real opportunity here to set up a PR company and advise these people. Instead of talking to them on the phone and giving them the information for nothing, I could actually charge them for it.

'I had no idea how to start my own business. When I look back I can't believe I did it! I had no business plan, no thought of how I was going to pay for anything, no discussions with the bank, nothing! I asked a colleague, Judith, if she wanted to come and work with me. I wrote to some companies and got one to say that they would see me, and that led to quite a lot of work from them. I set up offices above a second-hand bookshop, employed a secretary, and Judith and I drove all over the place trying to get business. It just grew! I think, looking back, that the reason we were successful is that I didn't have any criteria on which to judge myself, I just did the best I could. I think it's harder these days to start a business because of all the research and feasibility studies that you are asked to do and all the legislative requirements. I think it puts people off, it can feel too hard and the business can be analysed to death before anything begins. It may all become too technical and way too scary. It's a bit like having children – if you were to weigh up the costs in time and money that having children takes, you wouldn't enter into it because it all seems too much!

'What happened with me is that I used true entrepreneurial spirit. I had a vision, my enthusiasm and commitment. But I couldn't even read a set of accounts. I had no idea if we were making money, which is absolutely frightening. I started with a blank sheet of paper and went where my gut feelings told me to go. To be fair, though, I worked all the hours under the sun to make it work.'

It always intrigues me what happens in a family when both parents are working extremely hard. I wonder how it all fits together and if you can work as hard as that and have a truly happy and balanced home life. When home was mentioned Sarah was more cautious with her recollections. I sensed that not everything went as well as the adventure of her business starting. To begin with Sarah didn't feel comfortable sharing the intimate pain of her personal life, but she changed her mind as she felt it was important for others to read and maybe learn from.

'Back at home is really a bad bit of the story,' she explained. 'Basically, what happened is that the girl who was my nanny had moved into our family home, as we had moved house by this stage. I worked away from home a lot and it had reached a point where my husband wasn't entirely happy with me working so hard and being away so much, but he respected my need to do what I wanted to for my business. And to be fair (this sounds like I'm making excuses), we enjoyed a very good lifestyle: my salary was better than his and we were able to afford to educate our children privately and experience worldwide holidays, which I think is important. So from that point of view everything was hunkydory. But underneath all of this my husband was becoming increasingly unhappy with the fact that I wasn't there and, to be blunt, ended up having a relationship with the nanny, because she was at home and she was in effect the 'wife'. I was rarely there and was unaware of this 'relationship' at the start. When I found out I decided to accept the situation and continue to live in the same house, but lead separate lives as I felt at the time that it was best for everyone, mainly the children. My husband and the nanny were very discreet when I was at home and this arrangement continued for another ten years until our children had grown up. We are now divorced.

'I ask myself if the business was to blame for the break-up of my marriage. My answer is that I don't know. I think it would be very simplistic to say that it was. I suspect that what happened was that two fairly intelligent people got married, had children and just gradually grew apart, as a lot of people do. We were both busy with our own agendas and we didn't spend enough time on our relationship. A good analogy is that it's like two people being in different train carriages. The carriages are on the same track when they get married, gradually the tracks move apart and then hopefully they come back together again, but sometimes they go off in completely different directions. Our relationship ended amicably, although there was the odd fall-out over silly things.

'I do feel that I paid a personal sacrifice. I also think my children would tell you that they paid a personal sacrifice too, although children are so geared to thinking how they should think and feel that I'm not quite sure if it's how they really feel or what they think they should feel. My eldest daughter particularly feels that she got a poor deal and she has told me so, which hurts. I like to think that I have been there for them and have given them a lot of things. There have been occasions when I had the choice of, say, a school sports day or a business meeting. I would choose the meeting. I always put work first. That is being completely honest. I don't believe that you can be successful in business by being half-hearted about what you do.

'That's why I think it is tremendously difficult to have a successful home life and a successful career. I realize that some women do achieve it, but unfortunately I didn't have both. I have always felt that the people I employ are my responsibility; I have tremendous loyalty to them. They have mortgages and financial commitments as well as me, so I have to make sure that I continue to bring in the business for all of us to achieve financially. If that meant that while I was out chasing the business my nanny had to take my child to the doctors for her jab, then so be it. I realize that my child probably wanted mummy to give her a cuddle, but that was the choice I made and the price we all paid. At one point, if I got home after the children had gone to bed I would write a letter to the girls letting them know what I had been doing during the day. If I left before the children woke up they would write back to me, telling me about their day. That's how we communicated when I wasn't able to see them.

'My eldest daughter Emma did become wayward and rebelled from her privileged lifestyle. She ran away from home at 16 to set up home with her boyfriend, she took drugs and had to have an abortion. Now she is happily married with three children and very happy being a mum. She still says to me that she resents me not being around for her when she was young. My youngest daughter Sam adjusted much better and isn't resentful, she is more laid back and calm. I used to blame myself constantly for the problems Emma experienced and suppose I try to compensate now. I have found talking to other people that 'stay-at-home' mums also experience the same problems with their children, so I don't blame myself so much as it probably would have happened anyway.

'I feel the whole experience drastically affected me. In a business meeting I am always confident; however, in my personal life I lack a tremendous amount of confidence in myself as a person and in my ability to do things. I realize that other people don't perceive me that way; very few people would believe that, only people who know me very well. Most people only see the really driven businessperson, which is obviously what I prefer. What they don't actually see is the shivering wreck that is at home sometimes. If I worry about something I usually keep it to myself.

'About seven years ago the business went through a very bad time: one of our clients went bust. The last thing they did before they went bust is spend approximately £70,000 with us in a last-ditch attempt to get some publicity and market share. Unfortunately we were the third party in this, for example we were publishing and printing material so we had to pay the suppliers whether we got paid or not. It wasn't just our time we had lost, it was the third-party bills. We plunged into the red by about £60,000, which was money I couldn't even imagine owing. The advice I was given at the time was to go bankrupt, which I absolutely refused to do, as my name and credibility were on the line. We managed to trade out of the situation, although it took us about four years. So I've had very bad times and I've had very good times as well.

'What I learnt from this was to know where we are financially each month in terms of income. In today's business climate that's quite hard, as most people don't want to sign up to an annual contract, they want to use you on an ad hoc basis. I used to worry where the work was going to come from, but it always arrived. It's like a funnel approach: if you keep putting stuff in the top, it will come out the bottom eventually. I love what I do and I know I have made a positive difference to so many organizations and that's what keeps me going. I can honestly say that I have no regrets and that I would do it again if I could. I feel that I spent the first few years of my life living for my parents and abiding by their rules and values, the next part of my life living for my own family and ensuring that their needs were met, and now I am living for me and making sure I am living and working to make myself happy. I am working on giving myself the time and space to wake up and smell the flowers!'

I am amazed at Sarah's attitude. Even though her husband and her nanny betrayed her personal trust, she has learnt to overcome the resentment and realize that she cannot allow it to dominate her life. She has learnt to trust again and she surrounds herself with people she respects and trusts. She has realized that constant communication, being open and honest with her staff and customers, and allowing everyone to be responsible for their own clients and workload maintains her personal and business credibility and for Sarah that matters. Her motto is: 'Do unto others as you would be done to yourself.'

Since I first interviewed Sarah she has developed a sister company in South Africa, where she is now based. She has developed consumer market work, which has come about partly as a result of her own work within the fruit industry in South Africa, with opportunities to develop synergies between the two businesses.

Sarah believes that the people who have influenced her are those she has worked with over the years and her clients. Looking outside her business, she has always admired people with clear leadership qualities, and considers two outstanding people to be former New York mayor Rudy Giuliani and Virgin Group owner Richard Branson.

I asked Sarah how she defined the word 'success'. She replied, 'I think knowing that I can look at myself in the mirror every night, knowing that I have done my best and been honest in my business dealings, and knowing that I have gone that extra mile for my team and for my client. I am a great believer in leading by example and am much happier giving to others than taking for myself.

'What keeps me motivated is the tremendous enjoyment I get from my job and from seeing others around me growing in stature, knowledge and confidence. I have always loved my job and felt so sorry for those who have to drag themselves into work each day. My problem has been staying away! I see each day as a new challenge and wake up to enjoy it.'

I wondered what she loved most about working for herself. 'The fact that I have the freedom to come and go as I please,' she said. 'These days, if I want to take off to the Kruger National Park for a fortnight to go and play with the Big Five, that's exactly what I do, but never at the expense of a client or a member of staff. I dictate my working hours and conditions and there is great satisfaction from that. I have recently taken up ballroom dancing and often pop out in the middle of the day for a lesson, as there is less demand for teaching during work hours.

'What is most challenging is finding the right staff, whether we are talking about South Africa or the UK, and managing a UK business from South Africa while, at the same time, not interfering on a day-to-day basis. I have learnt not to appoint people in a hurry, to take my time and to carry out psychometric testing. I wouldn't let this testing alone make a decision, but it has helped me identify how best to work with people. I have also had to learn to be a much better delegator than I used to be – you have to let people grow in their roles and give them increasing responsibility, or you will lose your best people, those able to stand next to you and run your business when you decide to retire!'

When I asked Sarah about her scariest moment, she replied, 'Probably when, in the very early days, I realized how cash flow worked and found out I didn't have enough money to pay the wages. I had to make one team member redundant and I spent a week of sleepness nights before I plucked up the courage to tell her. Her reaction spoke volumes. She looked at me, got up, walked out of the room and shot back the comment, "You can stick your job up your ****'!" I wondered why on earth I had been worried about telling her for all that time.

'Or, I guess, waiting to hear the result of a pitch for new business. Everyone works so hard and gets so worked up to do the "best" presentation, and waiting for the news is terrible. Over the years you come to accept that you win some and lose some. You just need to win more than you lose!'

I asked Sarah to share the practical steps she would advise women to take in both work and home life. She said, 'Make sure your family know exactly what they are letting themselves in for, and if anything, make it sound more time consuming than it will be. You will need their support more than anyone's.

'Try to get your work and home life balance right. This is extremely difficult and something I wasn't very good at, always putting my effort into work and letting my family life suffer as a result.

Sarah's top tips

- Go with your gut instinct.
- Believe in yourself.
- If you believe in your idea enough, then go for it.
- Don't be put off by people saying no, keep going.
- Never be afraid to ask for help.
- Never be afraid to admit a lack of knowledge, always ask – being honest with people is the way to an honest relationship with them.
- Surround yourself with people you trust.
- Don't run before you can walk. Start small and gradually build up.
- If you have setbacks don't be frightened by them, be determined enough to believe that anyone who wants to get somewhere in life can get there. It may just take some people longer than others.
- Always behave in business as you would want others to behave towards you. It always pays off and you can sleep at night.

- Beware of the deadly sin of envy. Jealousy is a horrible trait. Revenge never pays.
- Research the market you plan to enter, and don't think that because you are doing something differently it will necessarily be successful.
- Listen. Just stop talking sometimes and listen to what people around you have to say. And take it in. It may not always be what you want to hear, but if someone is bothering to tell you, it is usually worth listening to.
- Learn as much as you can about finance and work closely with your accountants or your bank. Understand that cash flow is king, not profitability.
- Write everything down. Many a good idea is lost because you have it while you are driving to work, and once you walk into the office and the normal daily tasks take over you forget what it was. It's also useful to keep a pad and pencil next to your bed at night.
- Never mix business with your personal life. Don't have an affair with one of your staff and don't employ your friends. It rarely works.
- Lead by example: be the first person in the office in the morning, and the last home at night. You can't win loyalty, you earn it.
- Always reward and encourage your staff and never forget to say thank you. A few simple words, an email or a memo, can mean a lot to the junior who has stayed late to help out.
- Never take anything or anyone for granted. No one owes you a thing.

'Make a golden rule that you will get home early at least once a week – and by that I mean at 4 P.M., not 6 P.M. instead of the more usual 8 P.M. If you take work home at the weekends, do it in the evenings or early in the morning, or when your husband is engrossed in sport.

'I'm not really very good at strategy, I just follow my gut feel and go with what I think is right at the time. I've made plenty of mistakes but always tried to learn from them, and have never been afraid to admit that I am wrong.'

Making it Happen for You – Trust

What does Sarah do?

- Trusts herself.
- Earns trust.
- Trusts others.
- Avoids emotions that trample on trust.

How can you model Sarah and be trusting?

- Trust your gut instinct.
- Stand in other people's shoes.
- Delegate effectively.
- Remove negative emotions.

How trusting are you?

Think about what you really want to achieve in your business. With that in mind, score yourself from 0 to 10 on the statements below. A score of 0 means you really disagree and a score of 10 means you really agree.

- I trust my own judgement.
- When I make a decision I am able to live with it.
- I am aware of my gut instinct.
- I often use my gut instinct to help me make decisions.
- I am a person who can be trusted.
- If I ask someone to do something, I am able to leave them to get on with it.
- Others tend to trust me.
- I think trust is important.
- I get people's trust quickly.
- I always keep my word.

CHECK YOUR ATTITUDE

Add up your total score out of 100.

- *If you scored 85–100 points* – You're probably very trusting. To hone your trusting instincts further, have a go at the steps below.
- *If you scored 50–84 points* – An in-between score. See how you can tone your trust muscle and build up some strength. Work out with the exercises below.
- *If you scored 0–49 points* – You may have some issues around trust. Don't get all trussed up but triple your trust! Try the exercises below – trust me, they might help.

Three Steps for Developing Trust

STEP 1: TRUST YOURSELF AND GO WITH YOUR GUT INSTINCT

Have you ever had the experience when you've been asked to do something and you said yes, but at the time something inside was telling you to say no? Your stomach was churning, silently attempting to influence you. Why does that happen and should you trust it? That internal churning sensation, not to be confused with wind, is your gut instinct. According to Sarah it is worth trusting and I've got a funny feeling in my tummy that she might be right.

When we make a decision to do something, we rationalize the pros and cons logically in our head, in our conscious mind. But our conscious mind only accounts for a tiny fraction of our mental processing capacity. Enter stage right the subconscious mind. Whatever we do, our subconscious mind is busy at work in the background. It influences our decisions more then we might realize. The conscious mind can only hold between five and seven thoughts at any one time. It's a bit like the screen on your computer: you only see a fraction of what the whole computer is doing. The subconscious is like the processing capacity behind the screen, it's running the show. That gut feeling is based on the information held in both parts of your brain and it's a way of alerting you to stop and think.

The decisions we make are often based on past experience. Some of this we don't consciously remember, it's held in our subconscious. Whether you call it intuition, a hunch or gut feel, it's worth listening to because it comes from the sum of your past experiences. When you understand that your gut can serve a purpose other than digesting your food and refusing to fit into size 10 jeans, why not leverage the power of working with it and learn when to trust it?

Sarah trusted other people and sometimes they let her down. In these situations it would seem that it's her ability to trust her own judgement that has helped her to deal with the setbacks. When one of her partners went bust and plunged her £60,000 into the red, she ignored the rational, logical advice of the bank and carried on trading. She trusted her instincts that this was the right thing to do. This is the essence of inner trust. It's about making decisions that sometimes may not seem logical in your head, or to anyone else for that matter, and then sticking with them, because you know it's the right thing to do. As Sarah says, 'I can honestly say that I have no regrets and that I would do it again if I could.' How can you develop your gut instinct and know whether to trust it?

Exercise: Leveraging your gut instinct

First of all you need to get tuned into how your gut feeling communicates with you. For many people it's a sensation in the abdominal area, but instinctive feelings can manifest themselves in other ways too: your heart or other areas of your body. Look at the list of phrases below to give you some clues:

- In my heart of hearts I know it's the right thing to do.
- My head says yes, but my heart says no.
- I just knew that was going to happen.
- My head says one thing and my heart says another.
- Sometimes I let my heart rule my head.
- I've got a niggling feeling somewhere.
- I don't know why, but I feel a bit nervous about this.
- I want to follow my heart.
- I just know this is the right thing to do.
- A little voice in my head keeps telling me not to do it.
- I feel it in my bones.
- I've got a funny feeling about this.
- Something tells me I'm right.
- I get a sense that this is the right thing to do.

Over the next five days, notice if you get any intuitive feelings. Where in your body does the feeling come from? Think about intuitive feelings you've had in the past. Did you go with them? If so, did it work out? If you didn't, with hindsight was the 'gut feeling correct'. Make a real effort to get to know your instincts and where they come from. The better you know them, the more you'll be able to assess how accurate they are and use them in decision making.

STEP 2: GET THE TRUST OF OTHERS BY STANDING IN THEIR SHOES

Understanding and communication always open the door to the possibility of trust. And if trust is broken, having an understanding of what caused the breakdown can help you to move on.

If this is a trait you'd like to develop, here's something you can do to increase your ability to understand and communicate with others, so they are more likely to trust you. I'm sure women everywhere will love it because it involves getting a new pair of shoes!

Exercise: Getting some new shoes

To help you develop trust, start thinking about things from other people's perspectives. Ask yourself: 'What do I need to do, and how do I have to behave, if I am to earn the trust of those around me?' To help find the answer, look at things from their perspective by metaphorically stepping into their shoes. Here's how:

• Think of a person whose trust you want to earn.
• Draw an imaginary circle on the floor.
• In the middle of the circle, imagine that you see the shoes of that person.
• Step into the shoes and imagine that you are now that person.
• As you stand in their imaginary shoes, look at and hear the world from their perspective. Think about their view of the world. As you do, wonder what would need to happen for this person to trust someone else.

- Step out of the circle and become yourself again.
- Write down everything that you can think of that would help you to gain the trust of this person.

This technique is particularly useful if you undertake international trade. Sometimes cultural differences can cause trust to break down. Understanding can open up the possibility of trust again. Use the technique for staff, clients, suppliers or the bank manager.

STEP 3: TRUST OTHERS

How do you demonstrate that you trust someone? In a work situation, leaving people to get on with their jobs, without constantly nagging and checking up on them, is a good start. People who can do this are usually good at delegating. Here's a simple three-step guide to delegation.

Three-step guide to delegation

1. Agree with the person you are delegating to exactly what has to be done, when it has to be done and how it has to be done. Make sure you get a verbal agreement on deadlines. Ensure they know to ask if there's anything they don't understand.
2. Ask if they need any support with any aspect of the task.
3. Leave them to get on with the job. Don't keep checking up on them, that's what delegation is all about. Do this and they will feel trusted.

STEP 4: GET RID OF EMOTIONS THAT TRAMPLE ON TRUST

Sarah seems to have had her fair share of trust-trampling experiences in the garden of life. Despite this, trust triumphed. She remains open, trusting and not the slightest bit bitter. Envy and revenge are weeds that don't grow in her garden. Just as weeds are ugly in a garden, negative emotions are in life. Sarah seems to have strong underlying values of trust, respect and integrity that act as her own personal weedkiller.

Exercise: The triangle of trust

If you want to watch your garden of trust grow, this exercise will help you to pull out the negative emotional weeds. When you've identified negative emotions that prevent you from being trusting, you can make room for some more positive behaviours such as trust to grow.

- Write the numbers 1, 2 and 3 on three squares of paper.
- Make a triangle shape with the paper on the floor by placing paper 1 at the bottom lefthand corner of the triangle, paper 2 at the peak and paper 3 at the bottom righthand corner.
- Stand on position 1. Think of one thing that prevents you from being trusting. It might be a negative experience, a feeling or an emotion. Whatever it is for you, identify it in position 1.
- Give this trust-trampling emotion or experience a name, maybe Ruth Resentful – whatever you like.
- Step out of position 1.
- Move to position 2. Here you are more resourceful, you are the best you can be. In fact, here you are totally fabulous.
- In position 2 feeling fabulous, look at the 'you' who was standing in position 1 (I know you're not really there any more, but just pretend you can see yourself).
- Give the 'you' in position 1 some advice about what needs to change if you are going to remove your trust-trampling emotion and make some space for something a bit more positive.
- Step out of position 2 and get rid of the feeling from this position.
- Step into position 3. In this position you know everything there is to know about trust.

- Knowing everything there is to know about trust, look at the 'you' standing in position 1 and give yourself some advice about being more trusting.
- Step out of position 3 and get rid of the feeling from this position.
- Now go back to position 1. Look at position 2 and receive the advice that came from there. Look at position 3 and receive the advice that came from there.
- Take on board all the advice and notice how you now feel about being trusting.

At the end of the day, trust comes down to personal judgement and so will always be subjective in nature, dependent on the context and facts in a situation. By learning to tap into and develop your trust instinct, you may find you have a great new personal assistant when it comes to making decisions in your business life.

'Trust yourself, then you will know how to live.'
Johann Wolfgang von Goethe

Innovative

Think 'out of the box' when looking for solutions.
If you always do what you have always done,
then you will always get what you
have always got.

If you are looking for a solution, I presume you have a problem. Maybe you know that you want to work for yourself but don't have that 'brilliant idea', or you could already be in business and need to expand your range of products. It is time to read on and learn how to spring out of your box with fabulous ideas that really excite you.

Mentoring Moments

An organization I was working with ran an event entitled 'Mind Your Own Business'. As part of the event I was asked to run a workshop called 'The Big Idea'. I began by asking: 'What is a good idea? How do you know if it is truly unique and innovative or an idea someone has already had and it simply isn't viable – like edible cutlery or a chocolate teapot?' I believe that the key to a good idea is to see problems as opportunities.

I had previously met a man called James Gibson from a relatively new company, BinFix. His idea had come from living as a student. He described his shared kitchen as a hovel, with an annoying problem in that no one ever emptied the bin, because no one could be bothered to change the bin liner. James set about finding a solution. He created a triangular-shaped box that dispenses bin liners from a roll inside. On the underside of the box is a sticky pad so that the box sticks to the bottom of the bin. When the bin is full it can be emptied and a new liner is pulled straight out from the bottom of the bin.

Some of the best ideas are the simplest and very often they are not entirely new, such as a different way of packaging and marketing something that has already been created. And new ideas often come out of things that have gone wrong. The Post-it note® was created after a glue was developed for another purpose but proved not to be very sticky.

Entrepreneur's Experience

I am often asked whether it is possible to test the viability of a new business idea. Here is what I advise:

1. Identify a gap in the market.
2. Develop something to fill it.
3. Look at how much it costs someone *not* to have your idea, costs in terms of:
   - time
   - effort
   - quality of life
   - money

- safety
- legislation.
4. Do your market research, talk to prospective customers.
5. Put together a plan – a business plan/passion plan/umbrella plan.
6. Check the plan for viability.
7. Go for it – face your fear and dare to do it.

I am currently researching my next new Big Idea and hope to share it with the world soon.

⚥ Making It – Meeting Dawn Gibbins, Flowcrete Group plc

The pianist is playing 'Every little breeze seems to whisper Louise' on the grand piano as I arrive in Claridge's foyer. The décor and atmosphere in this posh London hotel are completely apt for the occasion being hosted that evening. I am shown to the ballroom where I am surrounded by orange decorations to complement the sponsor's corporate colours and free-flowing champagne. Quite how I got my invite to the Veuve Clicquot Award for Business Woman of the Year is still a mystery to me, but my job is to persuade the winner to agree to an interview with me.

The award was created by Veuve Clicquot Ponsardin champagne to commemorate Nicole Ponsardin, who inherited the company from her husband, François Clicquot, after his death in 1805. She took over his vineyards and from small beginnings created the internationally known company that now bears her name (*veuve* is French for widow). The award began in 1973 and each year tells the story of five women who are high achievers in business life. They are an encouragement and inspiration to aspiring women in the UK and since 2000 the award has also operated in Austria, Brazil, Denmark, France, Germany, The

Netherlands, Ireland, Japan, Sweden and Switzerland. The yardstick the judges use to find the winner is based on a profile of Nicole Ponsardin herself: achievement, ability to motivate, entrepreneurial flair, acumen, dynamism, enterprise, innovation, style, tenacity, struggle and charisma. Past winners include the late Anita Roddick, founder of The Body Shop, Ann Gloag of Stagecoach Holdings plc, Anne Wood of Ragdoll Productions and Barbara Cassani of Go Fly UK.

This year's winner is Dawn Gibbins, MBE, founder, chair and majority shareholder of Flowcrete Group plc, world leaders in specialist flooring technology. A tall, auburn-haired woman dressed in an orange trouser suit decorated with leopard-skin patches, Dawn bubbles over with vivacious personality and delivers an inspiring acceptance speech. She is most definitely a woman in a man's world – with professional women constituting only 15 per cent of the construction industry, she is on a one-woman crusade to ban the image of the builder's bum! Famous in her own area of business for being a 'what you see is what you get' kind of a girl, she leads with kindness not fear.

Dawn agreed to a meeting at Flowcrete's head office in Sandbach, Cheshire so I could understand her success and hear the story of how her business came to be. Flowcrete is the world's number two manufacturer of specialist industrial and commercial flooring. It provides the technology to make floors for hospitals, airports, stadiums, shopping centres and factories. If you shop at Marks & Spencer or fly from London Heathrow, you've walked on a Flowcrete floor. The company has pioneered floors that are sugar resistant, self-levelling, antibacterial, multi-coloured, anti-skid and more. It has almost 200 staff around the world in sales offices in Dubai, factories in Malaysia and the Czech Republic, a joint venture in Brazil and a newly bought subsidiary in Sweden.

Dawn runs the company with her husband Mark Greaves, whom she lured away from his lucrative job at Shell some 14 years ago. They make a good team. While Dawn concentrates on marketing, developing new ideas and getting Flowcrete well known, Mark runs the day-to-day operations and keeps his eye on the finances.

Dawn explained how the company started. 'Flowcrete began over 20 years ago with me and my dad Peter, an industrial chemist. I had got this travel bug before I started the business and I went hitch-hiking all round Europe. I worked for three years on the land in the south of France, it was great, but there was no future there so I came back and started to work with my dad as his righthand lady in the lab doing lots of technical experiments. My dad was working as a consultant designing flooring products for other companies. He was approached by an engineer from the confectionary company Mars, which needed sugar-resistant flooring. Together we designed a system. Dad was about to sell the formulation to Mars for £3000, which was nothing, until over dinner one night my mum suggested he go into business with me and sell it to all the other companies that need sugar-resistant floors.

'We found a small starting unit, 40 square metres, only dad and I could fit in, we had to build a little office in the corner. We were living out of the petty cash tin really at first, didn't take wages out for the first year. Then we manufactured the product to supply to Mars, the first order was £20,000 and that was 50 per cent of the gross margin. That was the beginning of Flowcrete.

'In the early days I was working from 6 in the morning till midnight, it was really exhausting. You put your all into the business. I hadn't got kids. I really wanted to make this business work, but I hadn't got any business training whatsoever, so I became a "home-grown manager".

I had to learn by doing, which was great fun, because you learn by your mistakes but you don't do them again. Doing the books, the lab work, manufacturing a product, doing the typing, selling and marketing – you had to be a jack of all trades, it was tough. What I started to find as we were running the business was that I was very good with sales and marketing and with the people side of it, my dad on the technical side. The business grew on a combination of the two, it was really balanced.

'The greatest thing we did was being able to buy property. I lived in a council house with my mum and dad then, but I was able to get a mortgage and buy my own house because I had a proper job and accounts. We were able to buy mum and dad's council house as well, and only three years into running the business! It was so satisfying: we were on our way up. We just about doubled our turnover every year: £40,000 in the first year, £80,000 in the second, then £150,000, £300,000, £600,000, and £1million.

'I did realize about eight years into running the business that I hadn't got a business plan, I was just reacting to whatever came in the post or on the telephone. I was a very passionate customer service person, always wanting to please the customer or the team; I'm one that wants to help people all the time. We found that if we didn't actually step back and say "Hey, where's my business going here?" we wouldn't realize our dream and we wouldn't achieve what we set out to do. You have actually got to take some quiet time and reflect on where you want to go and have dreams; it is so important to star gaze. In 1989 we had been running the business for about seven years, we were doing well, got to a million pounds, but we had got so many products, it was a very complicated business. If a customer asked for a product we didn't have, we would design it and then go on to the next one, so we weren't commercially exploiting what we had actually designed.

'I thought we needed to start looking at the business. I went off to Manchester Business School and did a Women in Small Enterprise course,
which helped with planned accelerated company expansion. I was really busy with the business and couldn't spend lots of time training so
short courses were brilliant for me. What I learnt I came back and put
into the business. One of the best courses I ever did was by an organization called TMI, Time Manager International, the trainer was called
Edward Sheldrick. The course was about looking at your life and your
dreams and planning how you are going to get there. Basically, you
will not achieve your dreams unless you have a balanced life, you are
satisfied in your career, you are satisfied at home and you are satisfying
yourself personally, so you block out portions of your time, in the day,
in the week, in the month, in the year. You shouldn't work too many
hours, like I was doing at the beginning of running Flowcrete, and so
you need to reduce stress, to balance. Edward taught you how to be a
pearl fisher. There are two types of character, a pearl fisher or a pearl
crusher, and it is all to do with positive attitudes. When you meet
someone you have got to find the little pearls in them, the little gems,
and not crush whatever they are giving to you. It's a way of life: look to
the positive side all the time, and even if people are coming to attack,
just keep calm and find an opportunity or a win–win situation.

'After I went on that course myself, I came back to Flowcrete (we had
about 50 employees then) and said, "Right everybody, you are not
going to work for two days." I hired a castle, got a temporary receptionist in, and decided that I would put all of my staff through the
TMI course. It was amazing. Ever since then everyone has gone on
the course every five years. It's just like a reality check, where you're
going, and it really isn't about work, it's more about achieving your life
goals. If you want to be successful in business, you have to take time

out to plan and think and fit it in with your life. I experienced some reluctance from staff to going, as some people believed they didn't need it. Their attitudes were amazing afterwards and they thanked me for insisting they went. Everyone gained value from taking part. It got people behaving in entrepreneurial ways: if they had a better idea of how things could be done they voiced it, were heard and many ideas were implemented.

'I also learnt about profiling my staff, because I believe in my people and that running a successful company is about having the right people in the right roles. The results of the psychometric profiling – and there are no right and wrong answers – made the staff realize where other people were coming from when they were communicating with each other. It really improved their working relationships and it was amazing how it got interaction and team spirit going.

'Around 1990 I realized I needed some help, I didn't have to do everything myself. I felt I needed someone who had worked in a bigger business or had studied and knew how to grow a business. So I recruited an MBA. The downfall of a lot of small businesses is that they think they have to do everything for themselves, when what's needed is a serious look at their own strengths and weaknesses. 1990 was the first time we did a business plan. We basically said that we want to be the UK leader and we had a plan of how we were going to get there, certain market sectors that we were going to start penetrating and so on, and it began to work. In fact, by 1994 turnover was up to £4 million.

'There was a competitor the same size as us that we really admired and we wanted to buy them out, but we always thought there was no way we could. After a closer look we decided in 1995 that we could. We bought this competitor and turnover went up to £8 million. By 2000 we had grown to about £10 million, in 2003 £25 million. We have just taken over another company and the business keeps growing.

'It is tough running a small business. You learn so much and I have become more and more confident. I was a sweet little 20 year old when I started the business and I was in the shadow of my father, but he was so proud of me and he pushed me. He would say, "Come on, you can do it darling, you go out and be yourself, you can do it." I do feel really sad that my father isn't here to see all of this: he died in 1993 after just a year of cancer. He remained involved with the company until the end. The employees would carry him up the stairs in his wheelchair into the lab where he loved being. He was a gregarious showman, very unlike the "boffin scientist" stereotype that many people have in mind. He would have been so proud.

'It was my dad's illness that got me thinking about the environment in which we live and work. My thoughts were compounded when we wanted to move factories in Kuala Lumpur. The staff refused to move until I had done an energy audit in the new premises that we were moving to. I now know this to be practising the art of Feng Shui, which is an ancient Chinese cultural practice that advocates living in harmony with the environment, enabling you to move in tune to the patterns and vibrations of the energy around you. This in turn attracts abundance in life, not just wealth but health, happiness and prosperity too.

'I thought I'd start to learn it, but I wasn't really qualified enough to do the energy audit myself. We paid £2000 for a consultant, but since then I have actually studied Feng Shui and qualified as a practitioner. It's become a personal hobby of mine. I began to use it for a bit of fun in the business; now I recognize the value and it works. I've had a team of people audit all my premises, they came in and changed the colours and the lighting, cleared out all the clutter, added plants and ensured that everything was in the right place for the best energy flow. If you've got clutter around you've got stagnating energy, which blocks your mind and thought waves. It has had a profound effect on everything.'

I was very interested to hear how Dawn manages the balance in her life. Here's a quick run down of her working day. She wakes at 6 A.M., dons a tracksuit and sets off for an early morning run with her four dogs. She feeds the chickens before waking her daughters for school. She eats a healthy muesli and fruit breakfast before heading off in her bronze Volvo convertible with her teenagers to drop them at the school bus.

When Dawn arrives at work she plans her day and always has time to chat with her staff. She very often has a second run at lunchtime and eats a salad in the staff canteen.

At 3.45 P.M. she leaves work to pick up the girls from the school bus and heads home to cook tea. In the evenings she will entertain friends at home or use her time to give an inspiring talk to help other entrepreneurs.

'Life is easier now the girls are older,' says Dawn. 'In their pre-school days I was every bit the same as any other working mum in the country, dropping the children off at the childminder's on my way to work, and it's hard. I used to give myself some contingency time for those moments that always happen just before an important meeting, where the baby is sick all over you just as you are about to walk out of the door. I'm a lucky lady now as my husband does lots of the overseas travel and my mum is always on hand to step in and help with the childcare.'

From 2003 when I first met Dawn her business has continued to grow. Flowcrete inspires people across the globe who work or walk on its seamless floors. It now has 26 offices around the world and

8 manufacturing centres of excellence. Its 2007 turnover was £44 million with pre-tax profits of £3.5 million. Flowcrete has developed global brand recognition and stimulated a feel-good factor within its team so much that they all want to wear Flowcrete-branded clothing. It has also improved its communications, with a global newsletter being circulated monthly called *Our World* that keeps the team informed.

I asked Dawn if she could go back to the start of her business, what, if anything, would she change? 'The name,' she replied. 'I would not have called it Flowcrete, it's too grey and it sounds like flowing concrete. Everyone believes that I sell concrete and I own a fleet of concrete mixers, which is wrong. If we'd had a different name it would have been easier to grow faster and to clarify to customers that we are an innovative seamless flooring company.'

I asked Dawn about her inspirations. 'My dad was my biggest influence,' she said. 'He kept on saying to me, "Come on Dawn, you can do it." 'My mum has also influenced me with her caring, sharing attitude, and my team with their constant inspiration and ideas. Feng Shui influenced me in a big way, this was the real catalyst of cultural change at Flowcrete.'

How does Dawn define the word 'success'? 'Success to me is achieving or should I say exceeding your goals,' she said. 'Goals must be measurable to stimulate a feel-good factor inside. Our goals for Flowcrete are to achieve over 90 per cent employee satisfaction and 80 per cent customer satisfaction.

'People and their crazy ideas, their passion to get things right, that's what keeps me motivated. I love the freedom and independence involved in working for myself. Cash flow and juggling cash and profits are the most challenging for me, so I have employed the best accountants and tip-top managers to work in harmony in implementing our strategy to be operationally excellent.'

Dawn has recently sold Flowcrete Group plc and is now starting again from scratch. Dawn has set up an entrepreneurial holding company called 'Barefoot Living Ltd' which will develop a range of lifestyle businesses to enhance peoples lives. Dawns first mission is to make seamless flooring the vogue in homes.

Dawn's advice to women entrepreneurs

- Just do it. Go for it. It is the best thing I have ever done in my life.
- My motto in business is 'Dare to be different'. You must make sure that you stand out from the crowd with your products and services.
- Remember, self-promotion is not a sin!
- Ensure that you set up flexible working practices so you can use them as well as the staff.
- Ensure that you follow my Mars bar management theory – work, rest and play … Make sure you have harmony in your life; if not you will feel depressed.

Dawn's best strategies

- Operational excellence – deliver what we promise.
- Focus on the FLOORZONE – generate high-value specifications with specifiers and clients.
- Service applicators to maximize reciprocal business.
- Brand development – both company brand globally and product brands in the relevant markets.

Dawn's top tips

- *Dream* – visualize where you want to be in 5–10 years' time and then make it happen. Make your dreams a reality.
- *Dare to be different* – stand out from the crowd and get noticed.
- *Discover* – yourself, your strengths and weaknesses. Focus on your strengths.
- *Develop* – your team and yourself. Constantly invest in your people.
- *Do* – stop talking about it, do it.
- Teach your team to *TLC* – Think Like Customers, Talk Like Customers.
- *MBE* – Make Business Enjoyable.
- *TEAM* – create an amazing team, Together Everyone Achieves More.
- *KISS* – Keep It Short and Simple, don't overcomplicate your company.
- What gets measured gets done – set clear and time-bound targets.

Making It Happen for You – Innovative

What did Dawn do?

- Used the wishes of others to create great ideas.
- Gave herself time to be creative.
- Harnessed the power of synergy.

How can you model Dawn and be innovative?

• Make a 'wish list'.
• Create 'star-gazing time'.
• Get synergistic with others.

How innovative are you?

Think about how you generally behave when it comes to creativity and problem solving. With that in mind, score yourself from 0 to 10 on the statements below. A score of 0 means you really disagree and a score of 10 means you really agree.

• People often accuse me of day dreaming.
• I have a very active imagination.
• People often ask me for my ideas.
• I always seem to have lots of solutions to problems.
• I am always thinking of ways things could be improved.
• I have an open mind.
• The voice in my head encourages my ideas rather than criticizing them.
• I see opportunities rather than problems.
• I don't have a great need for structure.
• I always seem to be having ideas.

CHECK YOUR ATTITUDE

Add up your total score out of 100.

• *If you scored 85–100 points* – You are indeed the embodiment of creativity. Use the exercises below to get your innovative streak soaring even higher. Why not aim to get it off the chart?

- *If you scored 50–84 points* – Your creativity is plugged in for action. You're raring to go. If you want even more light-bulb moments, try out the three steps to becoming even more innovative.
- *If you scored 0–49 points* – Your creative juices are bit lukewarm. Heat them up and get them bubbling with the top tips below.

Three Steps to Become More Innovative

Coming up with the next great idea to make a million is everyone's dream, isn't it? We all want to find the goose that lays the next big, fat, golden business egg. Sometimes the best ideas are the simplest and why shouldn't you be having them?

The problem with ideas is that when we try to force them out we get mental constipation. The harder we try, the less we achieve. This can leave us feeling frustrated, fed up and red in the face. So what can we learn from Dawn, mistress of innovation, to help us squeeze out the perfect idea?

What is clear from her story is that Dawn draws inspiration not just from herself, but from those around her. By listening to the wishes of others, she's been able to come up with truly innovative products and very creative approaches to operating her business. The original idea that got the company up and running came from Mars Confectionery, in the form of a wish. Mars wished it could have a sugar-resistant floor. Like a combination of the Christmas Fairy and Harry Potter, Dawn and her dad worked their wishcraft. Abracadabra, as if by magic, the elusive sugar-resistant flooring appeared in a puff of smoke from the workshop. Flowcrete was conceived.

The Fairy Godmother approach to innovation is more prolific than you might think. When Mandy Haberman wished that she could find a baby cup that didn't leak, the result was the Anyway Up Cup. This is now a standard-issue item in any house with a child under 5. Sarah Tremellen set up Bravissimo when she wished she could find a bra to fit after the birth of her first baby. I could go on, but in true fairy god-mother style I'll stop my discussion of wishes at the customary, magical number three. Who knows, with just the wave of a wand, you too could be the proud owner of a great new innovation. Close your eyes and click your heels together three times, Dorothy. You're off to see the Wizard – the Wizard of Wishes, who resides in your imagination.

STEP 1: CREATE A WISH LIST

Open up your thinking to some new ideas by making some wishes. As you follow the yellow brick road to innovation, who knows what might be waiting somewhere over the rainbow.

Exercise: Wish list

Make a wish list, which can contain anything you want. Here are a few suggestions to get you started. Write down:

- All the things you wish you had but they don't exist.
- All the things you wish you could do but there's no equipment.
- All the things you wish you could fix.
- All the things that other people wish for.

Write down anything you like, don't be constrained in any way. A wish by its very nature doesn't need to be tightly defined or evaluated. Anything is possible. As you wish away, bear in mind that every single thing that exists in the world today began with a wish: the chair you're sitting on, the computer on your desk, the book you're reading.

They all began with someone's desire to create something that didn't exist. Work out your wishes and, like a rabbit out of a hat, who knows what innovations might magically appear in your life.

STEP 2: CREATE STAR-GAZING TIME

If you want to have great ideas you have to give yourself time and space to think. As Dawn says: 'You have actually got to take some quiet time and reflect on where you want to go and have dreams; it is so important to star gaze.'

You can solve mental constipation by dedicating time to considering where you are going with your business and giving your brain space to create. In certain states your brain becomes more creative. It operates at four different levels: you are either wide awake, relaxed, in a light sleep or a deep sleep (or you're dead, not a good creative state so we won't talk about that one). At each level you have different brain-wave patterns. When you are in a very relaxed state you have alpha brain waves, and when you are in a light sleep theta brain waves. When it's in the alpha or theta state, your brain has a heightened sense of creativity. If you want to get more creative ideas, don't try to push them out. Instead, give yourself a mental enema. Relax and let go, get yourself in the right mental state and see what amazing ideas pop out all by themselves. If you put aside a little bit of time every day to think and dream about new ideas, it can pay great dividends. Here's one way of doing it, but you can get creative about what works best for you.

Innovation toolkit: Star gazing

Set aside ten minutes every day for star gazing. Do a 30-second review of where you want to be, or of any problem that you have to solve. Play some soothing music in the background. Many classical tracks will trigger your theta brain-wave patterns. Sit in a comfortable place and just let go. Perhaps look at the clouds, the grass, the pattern on the couch. Close your eyes if that feels more comfortable. Welcome whatever thoughts float into your head, give your brain free rein to play with them.

After ten minutes in this relaxed state, jot down any inspirations in a 'star-gazing journal'. Then just carry on with your day. Be safe in the knowledge that your subconscious will still be at work, brewing up ideas to be revealed later, perhaps when you're snugly tucked up in bed.

Innovation toolkit: Keep a dream diary

Do you ever find that you have some of your best ideas just before you go to sleep? Then, like a one-night stand, they're gone without a trace in the morning. Your brain is in a truly creative state when you're just about to go to sleep and also while you are sleeping. The inventor of the sewing machine got the inspiration for the machine's needle when he dreamt about a tribe of Native Americans dancing around him, jumping backwards and forwards with long pointy spears that had holes at the top. Who knows what innovations you might be missing out on while you're asleep.

Always have your star-gazing journal by the side of your bed. Let it double as your dream diary. Every night before you go to sleep, ask yourself for creative answers to puzzling questions and problems. If they come to you in the night, get them down in your journal as soon as you wake up.

Step 3: Get synergistic with others

Dawn clearly uses the powers of synergy to create fabulous innovations. In her case 1 + 1 definitely = 3. When it comes to creating new ideas, being collaborative and synergistic is a winning strategy. History shows time and time again that listening to someone else's take on a issue can often lead you down a road to riches that you'd never have travelled using the power of only your own imagination and thinking. By combining your ideas with other people's you can come up with all sorts of things. Even what seems to be a tragic idea to one person can be transformed into a terrific one with someone else's input. A dead end idea can be turned into a four-lane motorway heading straight to success.

Take Silly Putty, a bestselling children's play item. It was invented by a scientist at General Electric who was trying to develop a new form of rubber for tyres in the 1940s. It went a bit wrong and the resulting material was what is now manufactured as Silly Putty all over the world. But it took a toy manufacturer to see the mistake as a possibility. Over 300 million Silly Putty eggs have been sold since 1950 and the product is now found in toy boxes, playrooms – and places mothers would rather not see it – in houses everywhere.

Dawn is able to get this synergistic effect by enhancing her own creative powers through combining her thoughts with the ideas of others. For example, she uses the ideas of her employees to kindle the fire of innovation in the workplace. She often takes on board their thoughts and suggestions. She says, 'If they [the employees] had a better idea of how things could be done they voiced it, were heard and many ideas were implemented.' Like flowers, you sow one seed and before you know it, you've got a whole garden. By collaborating with others in many aspects of her business, Dawn has fuelled her own creativity and imagination, which has led to the production of leading-edge products.

One of the best ways of combining the ideas of a number of people is brainstorming. The ideas that come from group brainstorming will inevitably be better than those that just one person would generate alone. Try a bit of brainstorming for yourself and see what you can create with a little help from your friends.

Innovation toolkit: Brainstorming

You need a flip chart and pens for this exercise.

- Gather together a group of up to ten people.
- Select one person to act as scribe.
- Define the problem you are trying to solve – ideally send this definition of the problem out to all participants prior to the session.
- In ten minutes write down as many ideas as the group can think of about the challenge in question. Don't evaluate the ideas at this point, write down all of them. No idea is too crazy, too stupid or too expensive. The goal here is to get down as big a list as possible – you're looking for quantity not quality. Size really does matter!
- At the end of ten minutes, categorize the ideas, putting similar ones together.
- See if there is one idea you want to choose.

To generate even more ideas, reignite the group's energy by trying the 'what if' technique. Add a 'what if . . .' before you brainstorm ideas. For example, 'What if anything was possible?' 'What if we had all the right materials to do this?' 'What if the sky was green?'

Another way to generate ideas is to look at things from a different perspective. What ideas would Superman have, for example? I once ran a brainstorming session with Wonder Woman, Cat Woman, the Bionic Woman and Spiderman all in the same room. It was great fun and we came up with fabulous, funky ideas.

If you want to increase your innovation levels, work with others. Great ideas usually come from a combination of thoughts. A spark leads to a fire. Remember to let your brain relax, so it can be at its creative best. And of course, be careful what you wish for, because you might just get it.

'Happiness lies in the joy of achievement and the thrill of creative effort.'
Franklin D. Roosevelt

To aim high

Good better best
Never let it rest
'Til your good is better
And your better best.

Traditional, anon

Mentoring Moments

I spend some of my most satisfying working time on a one-to-one basis helping clients to think out of the box and to be a sounding board for new ideas. When I first met Bex Knight she was already working for herself in business with her mother. Bex had some firm ambitions and dreams of her own and was ready to branch out with her new business baby.

'Note to Self' is her new creation, with a series of funky products and a book to complete the range. Bex is a hypnotherapist and a specialist in positive thought techniques. She knew there was a market for self-development books, so she coupled that with a gift book idea, aimed it at the 16–35 age group and developed a unique set of products. As we began talking about her ideas and I read her book, which is a very young and trendy way of giving positive affirmations, I realized that she was heading down certain routes to market. There were others she hadn't thought of that I shared with her. Because Bex is such a creative thinker, she needed some help in organizing her thoughts so she could prioritize them and put them into action. We wrote everything down on an umbrella plan (see Entrepreneur's Experience below). Bex then had a clear plan to work from and she is working through it at a fast pace, making decisions as she progresses.

We have had some really creative thinking sessions that I always look forward to. What has struck me is Bex's belief that people are people no matter what they have achieved. She will ask for help from people she admires without the usual fear. Before Anita Roddick's sad death Bex had been to a conference where Anita was the main speaker. When Anita ended her inspirational talk and asked for questions, Bex asked, 'Will you mentor me?' The reply was yes! True to her word, Anita mentored Bex and helped her to come to the point where she is today, in my opinion on the brink of something big.

Entrepreneur's Experience

I attended a one-day course called a 'discovery day' with a company in Leicestershire, Go MAD® Thinking. I had just taken two weeks' holiday and this was my first working day back. I thought that a 'disco' day, as my confirmation email had called it, seemed just the right way to ease myself back into work gently. I had gone along with an open mind; as a trainer it is always good to give yourself some time to develop different ideas.

It only took the first half an hour before pennies began to drop as to why successful people are just that, successful. The founder of Go MAD® (Go Make A Difference) Thinking, Andy Gilbert, explained the principles and I was intrigued.

The main thing I have taken from the workshops and his books is the way to organize possibility thinking into an umbrella plan. In turn, I have helped new businesses begin their informal business plan with an umbrella plan – and it works. Oh, and I also learned a new song, to the tune of 'I'd like to teach the world to sing': 'I'd like to teach the world to think-in a solution-focused way'!

I have Andy's kind permission to share with you the basics of the Go MAD® approach. In 1998, he began research into the question: 'What is the simplest way of explaining the success process that people naturally use when making a difference?' Andy and his team interviewed vast numbers of people in the UK who had already 'made a difference'. There were no criteria for specifying what the difference should be. Hence the differences encompassed a wide range of successful activities: commercial, career, balanced lifestyle, political, family, community, educational, personal relationships and many more. Some differences were on a large scale, others were much smaller. All were significant to the individuals making the difference.

By the end of the year Andy and his team had gathered an incredible amount of information from a diverse range of sources, all of which related to how individuals successfully made a difference. What they discovered is not a process but a thinking system. The Go MAD® Thinking System is a practical and easily understandable framework for success comprising seven key principles.

The team tested the Go MAD® key principles in a variety of ways. Pilot Go MAD® courses were delivered in schools for students and teachers and in business for managers. The team began helping more and more people to apply the seven key principles consciously and they started to realize that these could increase the probability of success in any area: business improvement, sporting performance, health and fitness, education, financial security, career development – the list is endless.

Here is a diagram of the Go MAD® Framework.

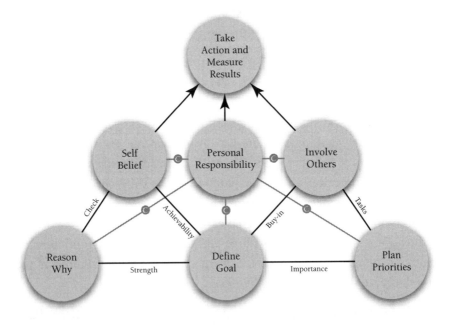

Remember, as a system, all the elements (key principles) have to be in place. If one element is weaker or missing the probability of success will be diminished. To increase your probability of success, ensure you apply each key principle. This Go MAD® Thinking tool called a 'bubble diagram' will help you to quickly and creatively generate hundreds of potential ideas. Give yourself a time limit – we would suggest anything from 5 to 30 minutes. Consider all the ten possibility areas writing down the possibilities generated. Move from bubble to bubble in any order and back and forth capturing your thoughts and ideas. Keep going until you have reached your time limit or increase the time limit if you still have more ideas to capture.

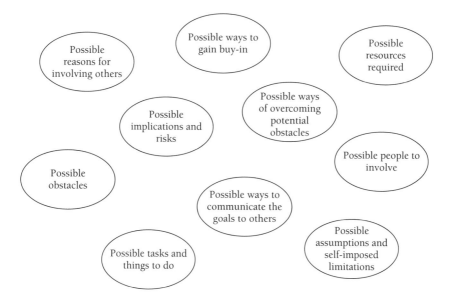

When helping people to develop an umbrella plan to organize their thinking into a business plan, I use the possibility thinking and visualization techniques, then draw an umbrella on a huge sheet of paper. For each area that needs to be addressed there is a separate section on the umbrella. This enables you to keep in sight the bigger picture while getting into the details.

To find out how the Go MAD® Thinking System can help you, log onto www.makingit.biz and follow the link to www.gomadthinking.tv/makingit.

☥ Making It – Meeting Perween Warsi, S & A Foods

Allison and I had arranged to meet Perween at her factory premises in Derby. Perween began her business as a 'kitchen table mumpreneur' when her two sons were young. She loved seeing the delighted faces of people eating the food she had prepared for them and wanted to take this a stage further. She developed her passion for cooking for family and friends into making dishes for the local Indian takeaway restaurant. This was fine as an interim measure to her bigger picture – the dream of owning a large food-manufacturing company. Today her company employs approximately 900 people and Perween has thrived on quality, vision, innovation and respecting herself and the people in her life – her customers, employees, suppliers and, more importantly, her family and friends.

Her values were apparent when our first meeting was cancelled at short notice. When we did arrive for the second scheduled meeting, as mums ourselves we fully understood Perween's reason for the postponement. Her first granddaughter had just been born. Family is Perween's first priority, therefore her secretary cancelled all appointments for a week so she was available to spend time and support her son, his wife and their beautiful new daughter.

Arriving at the gate house to S & A Foods and chatting to the security man and later to the main receptionist, it is clear that there is a high level of respect for Perween and the way she runs the business. She believes in investing in her people, the pillars of her success. She has established a learning centre for her staff where 75 per cent of her mixed-race workforce have taken NVQ qualifications and are encouraged to learn new skills, including promoting women into management, computer skills and language improvement.

The human resource team is encouraged to increase talent. They do this by team building, coaching and mentoring. They celebrate their staff as well as the company's successes through the following initiatives:

- A day in the life of …
- FBI – Fast Business Improvement.
- Think Big.
- Heroes and Stars.
- MBI – My Bright Idea, where all staff are encouraged to come up with a bright idea to improve the company. The ideas are judged by a panel and the winner is given £2000.

Perween is clearly encouraging 'intrapreneurship' within her organization and she knows how to motivate, retain and develop her staff. She operates an open, transparent culture that works very well.

At the beginning Perween had a very clear vision of where she wanted her business to be. She wanted to achieve national distribution, see her products worldwide and wow her customers. She asked herself:

- 'How can I make buying my food easier and better for the customer?'
- 'How can I continue to excite my customer?'
- 'How do I retain the quality?'
- 'How do I keep it authentic and innovate?'

S & A Foods now supplies ready-made, quality Indian cuisine to various outlets. It also introduced the first 'curry pot delis' in Asda stores nationwide.

Perween's top tips

- Pencil in meetings with yourself – give yourself time to think and to plan.
- Seek the services of a coach or mentor.
- Ensure it is your values that drive you.
- Be yourself, your own person.
- Adopt a positive attitude. It is the food for your inner soul and provides the calories to keep going.
- Employ like-minded individuals who fit your company culture.
- Innovate.
- Wow your customers.
- Simplify your business.
- Delegation does not mean abdication.
- Keep the goalposts the same.
- Raise the bar.
- Promote your successes.
- If you don't try, you don't know. Give it a try, have no regrets.
- Keep the right mindset.
- Be clear what you want, it is easier to make a decision.
- Be intuitive, go with your gut instincts.
- Learn to relax.
- Remember, what will happen, will happen.
- Try your best.

When she began S & A Foods Perween was the only woman in her Asian circle of friends to have a business. She felt massive guilt towards her family as being in her position was definitely not the norm, but then realized that she had a choice and that she was doing the best that she could. Allison and I came away from our meeting with Perween totally inspired. She is an incredible woman with tremendous depth.

Making It Happen for you

What does Perween do?

- Defines her dream and aims high.
- Constantly raises the bar.
- Always has her dream in her sights.

How can you model Perween and aim high?

- Define your dream and shoot for the stars.
- Super-size your dream.
- Bring your dreams and goals up close and personal.

How high do you aim?

Think about the visions and aims you have for your business. With that in mind, score yourself from 0 to 10 on the statements below. A score of 0 means you really disagree and a score of 10 means you really agree:

- I have big dreams.
- I like to write my goals down.

- I believe anything is possible.
- I think it's a good thing to leave your comfort zone.
- I like to challenge myself.
- People often tell me it won't be possible to achieve my dream.
- I tend to be quite forward thinking.
- I like to have something to aim for.
- I have a clear vision of what I want to achieve.
- I have big dreams, but I constantly take small steps to achieve them.

CHECK YOUR ATTITUDE

Add up your total score out of 100.

- *If you scored 85–100 points* – Hang on to your rocket, you really are shooting for the stars.
- *If you scored 50–84 points* – More timid than tenacious? Get some more oomph behind the arrow in your bow. Use the exercises below to elevate your dreams to new heights.
- *If you scored 0–49 points* – Get out of your boots, broaden your horizons, dare to dream. Try the exercises and aim for the sky, who knows where you might end up?

Three Steps to Aiming High

Aiming high and having an end goal or destination in mind is essential for business success. I know I'm stating the blindingly obvious, but let's face it, if you don't know where you're going how can you ever hope to get there? Without clarity of vision the journey to success becomes an aimless day trip where the driver travels round and round in circles. Eventually, dizzy, lost, exhausted and confused, she screeches to a halt, gives up and wonders why she hasn't gone anywhere.

Far from driving round in circles, Perween is riding in a rocket that's taking her to the moon. She epitomizes the notion of aiming high. With a huge vision that is ever growing, she knows exactly where she's heading and takes strides every day to move her in the direction of her dreams. Just like her delicious products, her aims are a moveable feast: as one is devoured another new and even tastier one appears on her plate. She continually aims high, raises the bar and then innovates to achieve her aims. In the process, she sets new and higher standards for herself and for the food industry.

STEP 1: DEFINE YOUR TARGET

So how can you hitch a ride in the rocket that will ricochet you to the mouth-watering moon of your business desires? If you want to know the secret, stop salivating, pick up a pen and start scribing, because those of us who write down our dreams are more likely to achieve them. Like a homing pigeon, a guided missile or the arrow from a bow, you've got to define your target so you can hit it smack bang in the middle.

Exercise: Shoot for the stars

Are your dreams floating around in your head or are they written down on paper? Getting them into a tangible form makes them more real. It defines more clearly the destination you're aiming for and gives your brain something concrete to aim for. An aim that's not written down is just a wish.

Entrepreneurs tend to capture their dreams on paper. Some write letters to themselves about what they want to achieve. I've seen others write articles about their future success. They do this in a journalistic style, writing in the present tense as if their aims have already been achieved. Others have created extremely visual representations in the form of posters or collages.

Whatever method you choose, successful aim definition has three magic components. All aims must be:

1. Positive
2. Explicit
3. Present

Like spice, this trio of ingredients truly PEPs up your aims and takes them to a different level.

Think of one aim you have for your business. For example, you might want to become the world's best handmade hat manufacturer. To make this aim more achievable, PEP it up:

1. **Make the aim Positive.** Always think about what you *do* want rather than what you *don't* want to aim for. Your brain is a magnificent but complicated organ and telling it what you don't want to aim for can send it into a state of confusion. Imagine for a moment that I asked you not to do something. For example, I ask you not to think about a steaming hot plate of Perween's delicious curry. What did you just do? You thought about a steaming hot plate of Perween's delicious curry, didn't you? I wouldn't be surprised if you're even salivating. In order not to think about something your brain first has to think about it so it knows what not to think about. If this sounds like a waste of energy to you, then don't waste your brain's time focusing on what you don't want. Let it move you forward by focusing on what you do want. 'I want to be the world's best hat manufacturer' works better than 'I don't want to be a shoe maker'.

2. **Make the aim Explicit.** The more explicit your aim is the better. Get as much clarity as you possibly can. How many hats per year? What quality, by when will you achieve your aim? How many people will be working for you? Will you have a hat factory? Who else will be involved? What will they be doing? What will your turnover be? What profit will you be making? In the same way as you need an explicit destination if you're on a car journey, your aims need to be explicit if you want to achieve them. If they're not, how will you ever be able to measure your soaring success?

3. **Make the aim Present.** Instead of saying 'I want to be the world's premier hat manufacturer' say 'I am the world's premier hat manufacturer'. Then act as if you are. Treat your customers as if you are, treat your suppliers as if you are, and treat your products as if they are the best hats in the world. By imagining your aim in the present as if it has already taken place, you will find more ways to make it your reality and live up to your belief.

Take your business aims and write them out using the PEP guidelines. When you've done that, read each one out loud every day and notice how much more achievable and real they seem.

STEP 2: SUPER-SIZE YOUR DREAM

Some people don't like to state high aims in case they fail and don't achieve them. To save face, they focus on all the things that could go wrong and avoid dreaming of all the positive possibilities. Like spinning wheels on a car that's stuck in mud, this holds them back and keeps them exactly where they are.

What would it be like if you set your aims high and focused only on all the good things that might happen? Is it better to achieve 50 per cent of a big aim or 50 per cent of nothing? If you don't get there first time you can always have another go. Perween certainly super-sizes her dreams, visions and aims. If she hadn't aimed high and pitched to Asda, maybe she'd still be making finger food for a local restaurant. She's the first to admit it was hard work, but without her high aims for success would she have got there?

A great example of someone who super-sized his dreams is a friend and mentor of Lou's, Geoff Thompson. He aimed high and decided that he wanted to become a published author. At the time he was a factory cleaner by day and a nightclub bouncer by night, so he really was aiming high. If being an author wasn't challenging enough, when he allowed himself to super-size his aims he decided that he wanted more. As well as being a published author he also wanted to win an Oscar. Of course, at the time this sounded very far-fetched to his friends and colleagues. But guess what, Geoff's super-sized dreams have now become his reality. More than 40 of his books have been published. He is also a world-renowned martial artist, self-help guru and screenwriter. His first short film was nominated for a BAFTA. Geoff and his wife Sharon were guests at the sparkly celebrity dinner. Geoff didn't win, but they both enjoyed the experience. Geoff continued with his screenwriting career and the following year was once again nominated for a BAFTA. This time the end result was amazing – he won.

Exercise: Super-size your dreams

Whatever your dream is, why not make it bigger better and bolder? If you only have a tiny dream and you achieve it, what else might you have missed out on if you'd had the imagination to dream a bit bigger? The more dreams you have and the bigger they are, the more you will achieve. Go for it, be outrageous, think of everything that you'd really like to achieve and super-size it. If you're struggling, then here are some questions to get your grey matter racing and your imagination ignited. What would be the equivalent of winning the Oscars for you? Ask yourself the following questions to help you super size your aims:

- 'What would I do if I couldn't fail?'
- 'What would I do if anything were possible?'
- 'What would I be doing if I'd surpassed my wildest dreams?'

Now rewrite your initial aim to include these super-sized aims.

STEP 3: BRING YOUR DREAMS AND GOALS UP CLOSE AND PERSONAL

When people imagine their dreams and aims they tend to think of them as a long way off, somewhere in the distance. They are part of their future rather than their present. Something that struck me when I spoke to Perween was her ability to bring her aims and vision close to her. When she talks about her goals she sees them as being well within her grasp. She knows they are achievable, she can touch them: it's as if she brings them into her present. She's like her own personal 'dream catcher'. Every day she spends time examining her vision in detail and then takes steps to make it her reality. Why don't you? Then even the highest aims will start to seem near and achievable.

Exercise: Dream catching

Sit comfortably, bend your elbow and cup your hand. Look into the palm of your cupped hand. In it see a representation of your vision: a vision that has been achieved and you can see in detail. It might be a picture, it might just be a symbol or a shape, but whatever it is it represents the achievement of your aims. Notice the colours, the sounds, the smells that go with your vision. Notice how you feel as you look at this and take it all in.

Now bring your hand closer so you can see your success in more detail. As you look at your vision, ask yourself, 'What is one small thing I can do today to move myself towards this vision?' Then make sure you do it.

By aiming high you increase your chances of achieving more, so shoot for the moon and who knows where your rocket might take you.

'Per ardua ad astra' (by striving we reach the stars).
Royal Air Force motto

Unstoppable

*An unstoppable attitude with the very best
intention is the recipe for success.*

One of the best stories I have heard about being unstoppable is that of
James Dyson. The way he created the Dyson vacuum cleaner, took on
the Hoover brand and ended up a household name is phenomenal. He
had an unfaltering belief in himself and his product and wouldn't take
no for an answer.

Mentoring Moments

Some years ago I worked for a Minolta dealership as their trainer. One
of the friends I made there was Owen Whittaker, who was employed to
increase business through telesales. Owen was a resting actor and we
shared wonderful mentoring moments with each other talking about
our dreams to act, write books and leave our mark behind.

Owen was married to an actress, Lucinda, who was also resting and
unfortunately became ill with chronic fatigue syndrome or ME. She

was confined to home most of the time as her energy levels were low. Very creative, she bought a word processor and began writing novels. Owen and Lucinda were used to earning lots more money than they were at that point and they were getting very near the knuckle financially. Lucinda had sent her first novel off to a few publishers and soon learnt that it was to be published. She wrote many bestselling novels in the 1980s and was hailed as the next Jilly Cooper. Owen followed with two novels of his own. They have enjoyed their success and never looked back.

Entrepreneur's Experience

The father of all unstoppable people for me is Sir Richard Branson, who in his book *Screw It, Let's Do It* shares his lessons in life and business. He says:

'Every lesson I have learned has been as a direct result of these tests. They include:

- Just do it
- Think yes, not no
- Challenge yourself
- Have goals
- Have fun
- Make a difference
- Stand on your own feet
- Be loyal
- Live life to the full
- Nothing ventured, nothing gained.'

Making It – Meeting Deirdre Bounds, i-to-i

Deirdre Bounds' journey goes from stand-up comic to founder of i-to-i, with a turnover in excess of £5 million sending over 4000 people annually to work abroad on volunteering projects. She admits that her work–life balance isn't as she would like it to be and committed to spending more time with her 3-year-old son after taking part in the television programme *Wife Swap*.

'It all started from a trip abroad about 15 years ago,' she said. 'I became bored with living and working in the UK and decided to travel for the first time. After spending five years teaching abroad, I returned enthused, inspired and determined to give other people the same great opportunities I had enjoyed overseas. So in 1994 I put my money where my mouth was and created a weekend TEFL (Teaching English as a Foreign Language) course as an alternative to the traditional month-long programme.

'When I launched i-to-i 10 years ago, I had no idea of the amazing impact our volunteers would have on their world. Starting out as a one-person operation run from a Leeds bedsit, I could not have imagined that years later we would grow to employ 120 staff worldwide, with offices in Ireland and North America. Now as we celebrate our 10th anniversary, it's incredible to think that the children who received their first English lessons from i-to-i volunteers are now young adults, the schools that i-to-i volunteers built now hold classes of eager young minds and the saplings they planted in rainforests have grown into mature trees. With the support of all our travellers, our staff and the communities with which we work, I am determined that we will continue to strive to be innovative leaders in meaningful travel and TEFL training for years to come.'

The last time I had seen Deirdre was 15 years previously when the scallywag had tried to talk her way into my aerobics class for free, and we'd shared a few evenings out together with our mutual friend Belinda. I knew Deirdre had gone travelling and set up her own company, as Belinda was now her personal assistant. But I wasn't prepared for the dynamic and unstoppable person Deirdre had become.

I asked her to tell me how it all began. 'It started 10 years ago when I came back from travelling,' she explained. 'I left Leicester having been dumped by a boyfriend and lost my job, everything had gone down hill and it was a really bad time in my life. I was abroad for about four years. I drove a bus in Sydney and did various things all around the world, thinking that I would never come back to Britain, but I did. And when I got back here, I was a changed person. I left with very little self-esteem. I was a bit of an ego maniac with low self-confidence. I knew I had some talent but didn't know how to direct it, and so when I got back I wasn't bothered about finding a job, because I didn't know what I wanted to do. I certainly knew that I didn't want to go back into a big corporate business – that's not me, I can't play the politics of it and I'm not actually talented in a corporate way. I'm a scatterbrain, so I got a job as a youth worker because I had my best time teaching teenagers in Greece. I'm really good with them as I'm probably that mental age myself.

'I got into youth work and they were all really fascinated with my story – where I'd taught English abroad, how I got the jobs. I told them stories of Japan, China, Australia and finally Greece, which inspired them and they wanted to know how they could do it too. These kids were only 17 and back then it cost about £1000 to be an English teacher abroad, as the course lasted a month. But I knew first hand that you didn't need to spend the money. I had just needed some basic teaching skills and some confidence to find a job abroad.

'I had a dilemma: I knew I was a good youth worker and I was also reasonably successful as a stand-up comic on the Northern circuit. I went under the name of Deirdre O'Sullivan, my maiden name. I didn't know which career to choose, so I decided to see how far I could get with the youth stuff and use the comedy work as an understudy.'

As a first step, Deirdre approached Leeds Education Authority and explained how many school leavers wanted to learn how to teach English abroad. This coincided with the gap year trend taking off and she felt passionately that all children, not just upper middle classes in private schools, should have the opportunity. The European fund held by Leeds Authority funded Deirdre to write a course and teach it in 13 inner-city Leeds schools. She also showed asylum seekers and immigrants how to teach English so they had the tools to go back into their communities and teach them the language. This was an approach that Deirdre had never thought about, but quite happily went along with. This led to enquiries about how much Deirdre charged to write and deliver the course. She knew then that there was enough demand to give it a go, even though she wasn't a qualified teacher trainer.

People thought that the four-week course was too long, so Deirdre condensed it into a weekend, which she decided to share with the general public. She looked around for help because she knew nothing about running a business, and was one of the last people to be helped on the Enterprise Allowance scheme. The scheme asked for £1000 to be put in a business account, so Deirdre borrowed the money from her parents and began her business literally in one room, a bedsit in Leeds.

She comments, 'I had nothing. I put my first course on in Birmingham, because I'd been to visit somebody there and I was coming out of Spaghetti Junction at 6 o'clock one dreary November evening and

I looked around and I thought this city is so ugly, people have got to want to get out of here. I thought this is where it needs to be – that was my strategy. I contacted the *Birmingham Evening Mail* and started to barter for advertising space and ask for help. People really supported me. Total strangers would say, "OK, we can't put you in situations vacant, but we can put you in courses in the top righthand corner on that page." Everybody loves to help. I learnt that on my travels, so now I'm not afraid to ask for help and usually it comes back tenfold, much more than you've anticipated. I received 140 phone calls in my little bedsit. I filled the places on the first course within four days at £120 a course. I just couldn't believe that people would send me cheques, in fact I'd pinned up the first two cheques just so I would believe it.'

After this initial success Deirdre ran weekend courses around the UK, still all organised from the bedsit. People on the courses then began to ask her to organise work experience for them in other countries. She had kept her contacts in Greece so she agreed to look into it. The deal for overseas schools was too good to be true: free trained English teachers who would work for free, as volunteers! She found that the world was a bottomless pit of demand for native English speakers.

'I sent out my first volunteers and was paid about £500 for organising it,' she says. 'I came up with a price by literally a finger in the air: "What can I charge for this service?" People also wanted to be met at the airport. I found it was just about having the initiative to think: "Who wants this service? Let's go out and find them and let them know that I can provide it." The internet was in its infancy, so I got books and I faxed out to different schools to find customers who would want that service. There was a Russian school from St Petersburgh that came back and said that we'd like to visit your school! I went to one of the schools in Leeds where I was delivering the courses to sixth-form students and asked, "Can you help, these Russians are coming in two weeks' time and I need a school. Can I borrow your office for two hours?" I was told, "No problem." So these two Russians arrived in a taxi and I'm sitting there behind the head's desk. I gave them a tour round the school and they said, "OK, you can send us the English teacher?"

'I got to the point where I needed to move from the bedsit, so I approached the same sixth-form college. It was all a barter system: I said that I'd give them a couple of courses if they gave me a room. We were in there for a year and by the time we moved out I had three staff helping me to organize the whole thing and freelance tutors doing the delivery of courses. It was then that I took my first real risk of going into a contract for office space and being tied in for five years. I never borrowed money and I don't like taking that much of a risk, but I had to run with it. I signed a deal for 800 square feet of office space in Headingly, the student area of Leeds. That evening when we moved in the sun was streaming in and I sat back and thought, "You've made it." I couldn't believe it, I was so proud of myself, I had worked so hard.'

Business continued to flourish and within two years, with 12 staff, Deirdre moved again to bigger premises. By this time she was becoming more ambitious. She had met her American husband in the States and realized she could travel from Manchester to New York in five hours, so decided to set up there too. She found an estate agent who sorted out an office and apartment. The deal for the office was signed on 6 September 2001; five days later it was the 11 September terrorist attack. Her instincts told her that it wasn't the right time to invest her funds in America, as no one was confident to travel anywhere. However, by this stage the business was still growing in Leeds and i-to-i moved again to opposite the university – they were bulging out of their current premises and the university was full of students wanting the service. A year later they had 32 members of staff, which Deirdre found unbelievable.

'We were attracting really good staff because of the type of work we were doing and the type of business that it is, it's young, dynamic and an unusual business,' she said. 'When we reached the point where we were teaching the courses all over the place and sending thousands of volunteers abroad, I knew I had to get some good managers in. One of the best investments I've ever made was taking on a great process manager. I'm not a detail person, I'm just an ideas person. He came in and started to put measurements in place and make sure everything was done correctly.'

As i-to-i continued to grow, it was approached by Americans who wanted to volunteer abroad for a month. They did not want to come to the UK just for a weekend to take the TEFL course, but Deirdre stuck to her guns about no one travelling with her company unless they had taken it. The solution was to put the course on-line. The £10,000 investment put into this was a great move, as in the last two and a half years that business idea has brought in £1.6 million! The company had underestimated the volume of backpackers all around the world who end up teaching English. Now they can go to a local cybercafé and get a tutor in their own time zone. This is a 24/7 market that gave i-to-i cash to really fuel the business. Deirdre feels very lucky, as this one truly great idea took the company forward.

'We were very focused on the education market and gap-year university students,' she said. 'So what I wanted to do was expand the marketplace and make volunteering a niche type of product. We were the first to approach travel agents and did a deal with the student travel agency STA Travel. Our brochures are on their shelves from Liverpool to Los Angeles. We were first in the marketplace there, the first to have our volunteer travel advertised in travel brochures, the first to offer short volunteer placements. Being able to go for a two-week period really opened up the market place. Expanding our customer base over in Ireland was also a great move, as it was virgin territory there and we are doing very well. We then opened up in Denver, Colorado. I made a lot of mistakes with this branch as the distance was very difficult to manage. We had to fire the director there, I paid him too much and the contract was bad. Sometimes you just have to pay a lot of money to get out of something, and that's what we did. In America we are now based in an old church in Colorado. We are now looking at different sports ventures abroad, sort of cuddly animal holidays. There's all sorts of ways you can go, but they have still got to fit in with the grand architecture of i-to-i, which is doing something worthwhile abroad, because that's what's very important to me.'

Deirdre's company now trains about 10,000 English teachers a year, which makes it the largest volunteer foreign language training company in the world. It sends about 3000 volunteers abroad to help on one of its projects in 25 countries.

Deirdre realized that she changed a lot during her time abroad and wants others to experience changes for themselves. One of the biggest changes was to stop drinking. She had a problem with alcohol and drank too much, but she used to hope that the problem would go away. It was meeting a group of different people that she had never been involved with before that made her interested in the meaning of life.

'I remember I was talking to an American guy about something,' she explained, 'and I said, "Do you ever get the feeling that when you say something and you feel really stupid for saying it, can't get it out of your head, and you replay the whole thing over and over again, and you feel embarrassed and your self-esteem goes?" He said, "Let me ask you a question, Deirdre. If somebody says something stupid to you, how long do you go away thinking about that?" I said, "Well, I don't really, I have a laugh about it to somebody," and he said, "What makes you think you are so important that people go round thinking about you?" It just hit me and I thought that is so true. So the next time I made a *faux pas* or whatever I thought, "Who gives a toss?" As long as I haven't hurt anybody or harmed anybody I let it go.

'It was profound moments like that which highlighted the bored people I saw on my return to Britain. I'd stand at the bus stop going to the local swimming baths and I'd watch the people at 8 o'clock in the morning going to work, they looked so miserable in their cars. I had nothing yet it was one of the happiest times of my life. Then I knew that I couldn't continue, because I was not going to be happy for six years still standing at the same bus stop, that's not me. I had actually moved on mentally and spiritually and that was a huge life change for me. Anything is possible. If you ask and you get rejected, that's ok, at least you have asked. If you don't harm people in the way you ask them, that's fine. If you show some humanity in what you do in your life, people generally approach you more, but if you are arrogant nobody's interested. Arrogance comes out of fear and insecurity and there are days when I'm insecure, when I think I can't do it, and it gets to the stage where I've just got to sit back and think, "You can, you might need more help from people, but you've got it to this stage and you can take it a stage further." '

Deirdre defines success as having enough motivation to get up and go swimming in the morning, going shopping in Sainsbury's and not thinking about the cost of things she's putting in her basket, buying

herself a new outfit, sitting having a meal with her family and special time with her little boy, and not worrying about not having financial security. She relishes time with her husband and son, but openly
admits that she spends very little time with him.

'Frankie is at nursery full time, that's my choice,' she says. 'There are
days that I take off from work and it will just be me and him. I try to do
the motherly sort of thing, you know, going to the park, swimming and
doing a bit of baking. He seems well adjusted, he's got good child care
and my sister rolls up and looks after him when we need to be away on
business. I do feel guilty when I'm away, especially out of the country
and when my husband feels that I shouldn't go. I think Frankie is a bit
too young to notice, but the first time he went to a Thomas the Tank
Engine show and I was meant to be going but went to a business meeting instead, it floored me when he got back and said, "Daddy went,
but Mummy you weren't there." I got over it, but it was mentally noted
and I will try not to do that again. Business is the first priority in my
life, I'm not saying it's right but that's just how it is for me. I know I'm
very lucky, I've got a wonderful husband and a beautiful son, but then
I'd like to think that I'm smart enough to see problems happening and
change how I do things.'

When faced with problems Deirdre initially rants, raves and worries. 'If
it's a really bad day that I've had I just go home, take a bath and I'll go to
bed very early,' she says. 'I'll wake up and it's a new day. The day that it's
happening I'm sinking in it, it's all emotional and you can't make any
rational decisions. Another thing that I suffer from – and I don't think
I'm unusual – is resentment. I take it personally but the only person
that it's destroying is me, because they don't know that I'm thinking
about them. It's all in my head, so I've really got to stop and think,
"What was my part in this? Why did that person do that? Did I do

anything to cause that behaviour?" I think I find it difficult because I'm not from a corporate background; I haven't come with any processes or procedures that I learnt during my graduate training scheme or anything. When I look back I didn't have a bloody clue what I was doing, so everything that has been built has just been problem–solution, problem–solution, so I've done things the hard way, I suppose.'

Deirdre's advice to someone thinking about starting their own business is to ask, 'What is fuelling the desire? Is it because you think you have a good idea? Is it because you want to be your own boss and have flexible working hours? Is it because you are extremely ambitious and you want a global company? First of all, look at why. Once you've mulled that over in your head and if it's still there, I would suggest you go to your nearest Business Link or equivalent and sit with somebody who's got a bit more knowledge than you. You can learn all the practicalities such as doing a business plan, cash-flow forecasts, marketing, accounts, profit-and-loss sheets, balance sheets and so on. Ask yourself what you have to lose, even if you did it part time at weekends. I didn't have anything to lose; I wasn't a high flyer earning £60,000 a year. But that's not a reason not to do it. I think you just need to weigh up options and not throw caution to the wind, because business is tough. Find out as much as you can and ask for help. I can only speak from my own experience. I started out with nothing on the Enterprise Allowance Scheme and ended up ten years later with a £5 million business doing what I love and making a difference – it feels good!'

Since I first interviewed Deirdre a lot has changed. She has another child, a daughter, and she has appeared on *Millionaires Mission* where she and a group of well-established entrepreneurs were challenged with making an entrepreneurial difference in Uganda. Deirdre made a huge difference and made some good friends too. She has sold her business to First Choice Holidays for a reported £14 million and is now working with entrepreneurs in the Yorkshire area.

Deirdre's definition of success has changed and modified since the sale of her company: 'Success to me is an inside job, it is comprised of many areas; health, wealth, relationships and being a decent human being. Even though I have achieved great success financially I find that I'm happiest doing simple things such as reading' chatting to my husband, playing with my children, experiencing pretty scenery, helping others in charitable work.

'Now isn't that odd, you would think that once you've made money you'd be happy … well, I fight hard to remain humble with it all, as if I think I've made it, I get arrogant. There's plenty more to do in this world and chasing your dream is only one area!

'Success is not about feeling happy, it is about feeling happy about who you are.'

Making It Happen for You – Unstoppable

What did Deirdre do?

- She was completely focused and passionate.
- She ignored the inner voice that tempted her to stop.
- She found creative ways around all obstacles.

How can you model Deirdre and be totally unstoppable?

- Ignite your passion.
- Shed excess baggage – travel light, get rid of those discouraging voices.
- Learn how to get round road blocks.

How unstoppable are you?

Think about what you really want to achieve in your business. With that in mind, score yourself from 0 to 10 on the statements below. A score of 0 means you really disagree and a score of 10 means you really agree:

- Once I set my mind to something I always do it.
- I stay on track and I am not easily distracted.
- I have a clear idea of my goal.
- When faced with problems I usually find a way round them.
- I am very creative.
- I expect to achieve my goal.
- I'm not put off by other people's lack of enthusiasm for my goal.
- I feel great passion about my goal.
- I have a great desire to achieve my goal.
- It never occurs to me that I won't reach my goal.

CHECK YOUR ATTITUDE

Add up your total score out of 100.

- *If you scored 85–100 points* – You are quite unstoppable. Take a pit stop to recharge yourself with some techniques that might allow you to go even further, even faster.
- *If you scored 50–84 points* – You're probably stopping and starting and need a bit more oomph!
- *If you scored 0–49 points* – You really need to turn the key in your ignition so you can get going and propel yourself forward in an unstoppable fashion.

Three Steps to Being Unstoppable

Unstopability is a combination of things. You need passion, focus and strategies to manoeuvre round everything that gets in your way.

Setting up your own business is like being on a very long car journey. After the initial excitement of setting off, when you've been on the road for ages, you've got lost twice and you're stuck in traffic, you think despondently, 'Wouldn't it be easier to turn round and go home? What keeps you going, what makes you unstoppable?

Step 1: Put fuel in your tank and ignite your passion

Something that stands out in Deirdre's story is her passion for what she does. Passion is like rocket fuel, it blasts you to where you want to go. Imagine for a moment that you are undertaking your journey to your dream in a fabulous Ferrari. It's a wonderful performance car that will get you where you want to be in double-quick time. Great as this sounds, no matter how clear your destination, how focused you are on reaching it and how well prepared you are for the journey, without fuel you're just not going to move an inch. Deirdre knew she wanted to go places. As she said, 'I'm not going to be happy standing at a bus stop in six years.' How can you find the passion to fuel your journey to your dream?

Our passions come from our core. We're often passionate about things we really enjoy and that tie into our values. As we grow older, we tend to lose touch with our true passions. Life just gets in the way. What are your passions? Try the exercise below to give you an insight into what might put fuel in the tank of your Ferrari. Have fun with it and remember, anything goes!

Exercise: Things you love

In the boxes, write down or draw all the things you've loved doing at various points in your life. Be creative with this, it doesn't have to be a list. Use different colours, experiment, remember everything. You might surprise yourself as you get back in touch with the real you.

Things I loved doing, being and trying
When I was a child
When I was a teenager

> **When I was a young adult**
>
>
>
>
>
>
>

Now reflect for a moment:

• Are these things still important now?
• Do you still love them now?
• What would it be like to have more of these things in your life right now?
• The one million dollar question: If you were incorporating these passions into your life and business, what would it be like and what might happen?

Exercise: Uncover your passions

Think about your life now and ask yourself these questions:

• People always tell me I'm great at …
• What means a lot to me?
• What makes me feel truly like me when I'm doing it?
• What am I doing when I'm at my best?
• What's important to me in life?
• If I could have been anything in life I'd have been a … because …
• What really gets me excited and fired up?
• What are my true passions?

- What am I missing out on by not engaging my passions?
- How can I use my passions to help me achieve my business goals?

When you have the answers to all these questions, ask yourself the ultimate question: How can I use this knowledge to make myself unstoppable?

Step 2: Shed excess baggage and travel light

You've got your fuel, your tank is full of passion and that Ferrari of yours is ready to shoot off into the sunset. Before you do set off, ensure that you're not overloaded. You won't be going anywhere fast if you've got six suitcases, a travel rug, a picnic basket and a flask of tea strapped to the roof rack. Excess baggage will slow you down and could even stop you in your tracks. Imagine the horror and embarrassment of the driver whose luggage has come disengaged from her roof rack. As she stands on the hard shoulder surveying the scene in helpless horror, her suitcase is crushed by an articulated truck and a multitude of cars precariously swerve round her knickers and toilet bag, the contents of which are now scattered across the three lanes of the motorway. Don't let this happen to you: ditch your baggage.

Deirdre recognized that her baggage was her constant overanalysis of what people were saying to her. She realized that this was a waste of time and energy. She learnt that instead of worrying about and making meaning out of people's comments and actions, it was more beneficial to put them to one side so she could stay clear and be focused on reaching her destination. She learnt not to allow herself to be weighed down or sidetracked by issues that weren't important. There is a crunch point in the story when she realizes that re-running scenarios in her head about things that happened during the day was not a good use of her energy. She decided to take a different approach. As she says, she switched from playing the whole thing over and over again then feeling embarrassed and allowing her self-esteem to drop, to thinking, 'as long as I haven't hurt anybody or harmed anybody, let it go ...'

How can you let things go so they don't drag you down, hold you up or stop you in your tracks? First, you need to identify what record it is you play over and over again in your head, then leave it safely on the hard shoulder of life. Then you need to drive off and let it go, hanging on to only the useful bits that will assist you as you journey forward.

Exercise: Excess baggage

An example of Deirdre's excess baggage is, 'I suffer from resentment ... I take it personally and the only person it's destroying is me.'

Write down at least three resentments or worries you carry around that slow you down:

-
-
-

Exercise! Let it go

Now you've captured this on paper, try this wonderful exorcise to get rid of that irksome baggage. Banish the voice that harbours resentments, overanalyses and makes meaning out of conversations you've had with others. Do what Deirdre does and at the end of a busy day – just let it all go.

Sit or lie down. You could even relax in a wonderful bath with loads of bubbles. Notice in your body where you are holding the tensions of your day. Start at your toes and work slowly up to your head, paying attention to every part of you. Each time you sense any tension, allow it to flow out of your body and float away into the distance so it is no longer a part of you. Notice how you feel as it leaves you. You are freer, lighter and clearer. As you focus on your head, notice your internal voice. Acknowledge that it wants to help you and ask it to give you your learning for the day. What positive things can you take from today that will help you in the future? Acknowledge what it has to say and then let all the unnecessary words leave you. Imagine all the individual letters of all the words of the conversations you've had that day that you no longer need just floating away. You're clear and calm, ready for a good night's rest and a productive next day.

STEP 3: GETTING ROUND ROAD BLOCKS

It's no good having the horsepower and drive of an express train if you're going to get stopped in your tracks by a leaf on the line. On any journey a roadblock can stop you dead. You can't always predict them and unless you can think of a way round them, you could be stuck for a long time. This is where it comes in very handy to have satellite navigation in your car. It can see things you can't because it looks at the world and your journey from a different perspective. From the sky it can see things that you can't see on the ground.

When Deirdre became stuck she very often asked people for help. Like satellite navigation, she used people with different perspectives and different resources to help her get round obstacles. When confronted with the problem of conjuring up a school from thin air, an obstacle if ever I saw one, she simply asked one of the schools she was working for if she could borrow an office for a couple of hours. It worked.

Deirdre is solutions focused. Faced with an obstacle, she always believes that there is a solution to be found. As she says, 'So everything has just been problem–solution, problem–solution.'

If you hit a roadblock, ask yourself the following questions. Think of them as your personal satellite navigation system, your obstacle-busting toolkit, giving a different perspective and some new options for how to get round the block.

Exercise: Obstacle busting toolkit

1. If I knew the solution to this problem, what would it be?
2. Who else can help me to solve this problem?
3. Who else could do this for me?
4. What would be a good outcome to this problem?
5. What are my options here?
6. What resources do I already have that I can use to help me with this?
7. How have I found answers to problems like this in the past?
8. If I were at my unstoppable best, what would I do now?
9. What small steps can I take towards moving this obstacle?
10. What haven't I thought of yet that could be the solution?
11. If anything were possible, how would I remove this obstacle?
12. What other ways are there of looking at this?
13. How could this be turned into an opportunity?
14. What would Deirdre do in this situation?
15. What precisely is needed in this situation? If my fairy godmother granted me three wishes to deal with this right now, what would I ask for?
16. What good might come of this obstacle?
17. Who else has encountered an obstacle like this? What did they do?

18. What feels the best thing to do right now?
19. What will it be like when I have solved this problem?
20. Imagine you have solved the problem and are now in the future with the obstacle behind you, what did you do?

If you're going to get there, wherever 'there' may be, you've got to be unstoppable. In the words of someone who made huge contributions to the world of medicine:

> *'Let me tell you the secret that has led me to my goal.*
> *My strength lies solely in my tenacity.'*
>
> Louis Pasteur

Determined

The ability to recover from rejection, time after time.

One of the main things new entrepreneurs want help with (apart from finances) is how to sell their product or service. What you need to be prepared for is that you aren't going to sell to everyone. Do your market research thoroughly and know who your target audience is. If you are selling to your target audience the rejections won't be as great as if you aim to sell to everyone.

Get used to the fact that you are bound to get people saying no and it is all part of the sales process. When you have a track record, you will be able to analyse how many people/companies you sell to compared to how many you approach.

I was delivering a sales presentation to companies who had been trading for up to two years. Even so, these people said that rejection when selling their wares still really affected them. My advice to you is, don't take it personally. Sometimes they simply just don't need what you're offering.

Mentoring Moments

Simon Woodroffe owns the Yo Sushi restaurants and was a dragon on BBC2's *Dragons' Den*. He has also written *The Book of Yo*. I love what he says about rejection. Every time he gets a no, he punches the air as he knows he is one step closer to his yes. This idea has kept me going many times when I felt unsure that I could achieve my goal.

Entrepreneur's Experience

Two of my clients had previously owned a small shop and had loved working for themselves. They told me:

'We had not done our market research properly and had leased a shop in totally the wrong position for what we were aiming to sell. Unfortunately, the business closed and my husband and I went back to being employed. The entrepreneur in us didn't go away and we made a conscious decision to learn by our previous mistakes, take more advice and guidance and plan our next business venture properly.

'I'm pleased to say that with determination and a lot of courage we have taken the step back into self-employment. We are both determined to make it work this time. We have discovered that many successful business people have failures. Our independent specialist travel agency is now flourishing. We are still learning and fully intend to keep going.'

Making It – Meeting Fiona Oxley and Karen Wilbourn, Lello

Fiona Oxley and her sister Karen Wilbourn are truly 'sisters doing it for themselves'. They create and sell handmade cards in the UK and abroad. Their company, Lello, is a recent winner of the coveted 'Henries' award, which puts it in the ranks of the greeting card industry's big boys. Henries awards are given to providers of outstanding quality and service, nominated by over 200 independent retailers. With over 700 companies to choose from, this is a recognition that Fiona and Karen are deservedly proud of. However, success to them is how they conduct their work. They adopt the family approach by bringing their sons to work, where they have set up an on-site crèche. They also employ many part-time workers, mainly women on term-time contracts with students through the holidays. They have fantastic staff-retention levels.

I had been asked to go to a new lunchtime networking club in South Leicestershire. As it's very close to where I live and not the usual early-morning breakfast club – which incidentally doesn't work when you have made the decision that you want to take your children to school yourself each morning – I decided to go. There were only a handful of people there, which disappointed the organizers. I, on the other hand, was delighted, as I met Fiona and Karen's father, who told me all about Lello. What interested me most about the company was their child-friendly philosophy. I arranged to meet Fiona at their premises on a farm in Desford, Leicestershire.

As I turned into the drive leading to the farm, I couldn't help feeling really calm. There were sheep dotted around in the field to my right and from a busy road I seemed to have stepped into an oasis of calm. Fiona informed me that she and Karen had advertised for an investor for Lello, as they wanted to expand and move premises from the cramped unit they were in close to town to a more rural position. They wanted to continue to grow and knew they needed help with their cash flow, so they had decided that a 'hands-off' investor was the way forward. The sisters were surprised by the large response and had to interview would-be investors for the privilege! They felt they had found the perfect match, as not only had their chosen investor got the money they required and wanted to leave the decision making to them, he also offered them the building within the farm's grounds. It was a fabulous setting for a business and for children to spend time.

I asked Fiona what made them want to create the business and what it took for them to get where they are today. 'We didn't set out to own a greetings card company, it just sort of happened!' she said. 'After passing my degree in graphic design I had been employed in the retail design industry. I was made redundant after only a year and found it hard to get employment as a graphic designer as the industry was swamped. I decided to turn my hand to teaching aerobics, as I was already a qualified instructor. It was also at the time when step classes were just beginning to become fashionable. I approached The Prince's Trust for help and was given a grant for extra training to learn step, a loan for £1000 and a mentor. I progressed to own a studio and ran it very happily for two and a half years. However, as with any exercise craze, other people jumped on the bandwagon and my business dipped as new step classes opened.

'Meanwhile, the design industry had picked up and I went to work for the Sloane Group as a graphic designer. I had always kept my hand in with design work delivering small freelance jobs. I rapidly worked my way up and when I left, two years later, I was in charge of the Tesco print account handling £2 million initiatives. I was head-hunted by the Sloane Group's competitor, based in London. I wanted to continue working locally as I had met my future husband, so they set me up in Leicester, and I took up the role of director. I loved the work as it was challenging and interesting. However, I dealt with all the major problems as the buck stopped with me, but it wasn't my company, I was just salaried. I ended up working 18-hour days, 7 days a week sometimes, as there was always a deadline and Tesco was really demanding. I also got married in that period. I don't know how I managed everything.

'In the last 12 months that I was there I approached my sister Karen to come and work with me. She had always been in the reprographics industry and was really not enjoying it. When I ran my aerobics business Karen and I had worked very successfully together, as she had taught part-time for me. I knew that we made a great team. I am the initiator and come up with the ideas and I know I am good at that. On the other hand, Karen is very good at following through, making sure things are done. I knew we would complement one another. I also knew that if there was a problem we would be able to discuss it and move quickly forwards. Karen decided to join me and we loved being in one another's company so often, as we are really close. After about 12 months things began to go wrong at work, though. My managing director in London was beginning to show his true colours and Karen and I decided it was time to put a plan in to place to get out.

'Each Christmas we were taken to New York to see what the trends were. While we were there we visited a shop called Anthropology, an amazing lifestyle shop selling beautiful products. Karen and I were bowled over by its style and ranges. I suggested that we use the money I had earned as director to set up our own shop in Leicester, based on similar ideas.

'We went ahead and set up the shop in the centre of town, selling stylish homewares and gifts. We planned to set up our own design company above the shop and I asked one of my employees to design and make a few cards. At this point we were still working at the design company as well as running the shop.

'A freelance agent came into the shop to sell us his products, saw our range of handmade cards and offered to sell them in other outlets. We decided to take him up on his offer and set up commission payments based on sales. During this time Karen and I left the design company who employed us. We took a number of contracts with us and all the people working there came to work for me above the shop to continue to deliver them. We didn't have time to give much thought to a company name or designing our own logo. We came up with Lello, as it was the branding I had created as part of my degree course years earlier.

'We ended up in the same situation as before: working and being busy all the time. We had no time for us or our husbands, parents and friends. We asked my dad to analyse the accounts to work out what was doing well and what wasn't. It turned out that the manufacture and sales of the handmade cards was returning us the greatest profit. We had almost fallen on the idea by chance. When the shop lease came up for renewal, we decided to give the card manufacturing a go, keep the Tesco contract and ditch everything else. We also managed to retain all of the staff. For the first time we had breathing space to concentrate on only two things and do them to the best of our abilities. This didn't last long as after retaining the Tesco contract for ten years as a valued supplier, our services were no longer required almost overnight.'

This is the point where the sisters were ready to give up and close the business. They felt responsible for their staff and didn't know how they were going to sustain work for them all. They had also unspoken agreements with their husbands that their business borrowing would never jeopardise their personal assets. Fiona and Karen spent time worrying and mulling everything over and were ready to announce closure when they saw a television documentary about why businesses fail. The message they took away from it was that businesses fail when they allow the event of a failure to stop them trying and simply give up. The sisters made a decision to put as much effort as possible into the greeting cards business and see if they could make a go of it.

Make a go of it they did! The determination they showed to keep the company going was great. They rose to the challenge and Lello is a thriving, expanding business today. They kept their staff, employed freelance, commission-based sales agents and the company has gone from strength to strength, supplying to outlets all over the world.

The way in which Fiona and Karen have created unique working lives to combine their family values is of great interest to me. They both had baby sons within six months of one another and knew that they weren't prepared to compromise their care. After two weeks of Redd being born, new mother Fiona took him into work. This was against the protests of family and friends.

'I didn't see the problem,' she said. 'In the early days he just ate and slept. When he needed attention I gave it to him. When he was asleep I worked. I knew that I wanted to return to work quickly after having him, so I rested completely for two weeks. My mum was an absolute star and did absolutely everything in that time. At the end of the two weeks I felt refreshed and ready to get back to Lello. As Redd grew older I realized this arrangement had to change. By this time I was used to him coming into work with me and knew I would miss him terribly if too much altered.

'I was chatting to one of the girls at work and she told me that she was a qualified nanny. I asked if she was interested in changing her role within Lello and it went from there. We dedicated a room to be a child-friendly zone and she began to take care of Redd during the day. This worked so well as it meant that I could still bring him to work with me and have breaks and lunch spending time with him.'

Karen wasn't so lucky with the delivery of her son Angus, six months later. She was very ill after a horrendous caesarean section that didn't go to plan. Karen had made the decision to remain awake while her son was born, but unfortunately the pain block hadn't worked 100 per cent and she actually felt herself being cut. Angus was also born not breathing and the pair ended up spending two weeks in hospital. The family were all concerned that Karen was starting to suffer from post-natal depression and to this day Fiona feels that the reason she didn't completely get swamped by it was because she came back to work five weeks after her delivery.

'This might sound mad,' she said, 'but Karen loves her work and really felt she had something to get stuck into. She was still taking painkillers when she first came back, but she stopped and rested when she needed to. Karen also felt totally supported by the workforce who surrounded her (mainly female), who all helped out with Angus and took care of Karen too. She felt it was the emotional support around her that helped get her through what was a horrendous time.'

Angus now joins Redd in the crèche at Lello, both looked after by the same person. The sisters are also very well supported by the boys' grandparents, who all take turns with the childcare along with their respective husbands. The dads take a 50 per cent role in the domestic chores and childcare at home, which Fiona feels is paramount to the success in the relationships involved. Fiona and Karen ensure that they alternate going out of town for appointments, and that way one of the sisters is always there for the children. The upshot is that the boys as well as the sisters are incredibly close.

Because the company is so family focused this is extended to the workforce too. The majority of employees in the 'making' area of Lello work around school hours, term time only. 'This suits everyone beautifully,' Fiona explained, 'as the staff can work around their families, in turn making them happier at work. They don't suffer the "guilt" problem that many working mothers do, as they are there for the family too. It works for Lello because we employ creative students during the holidays and it fits in with us all, Lello would rather employ the right person to do the job and make the working hours fit, rather than the other way round.'

Fiona and Karen have had their fair share of problems but have been determined to rise above them and achieve a successful business and a successful home life. They have both learnt to take time out for themselves and schedule a weekly reflexology session to restore their energy for life's next challenge.

Why we like working for ourselves

- Loving what we do, keeps us motivated.
- The motivation comes from trying to build the business to a size where we are recognized as a brand. But more importantly, it gives us a degree of stability and flexibility for the future.
- Motivation also comes from not having achieved our goals, even after nine years.

- Working for ourselves enables us to have our children cared for at work. We have never had to put them into nursery and can see them whenever we like.
- It enables us to be able to have a decent standard of living and work with like-minded people.
- What we both love most is the excitement each day brings, no matter how unpleasant it may be at times, from seeing our product on people's shelves in their shops and feeling that we have both achieved something.

The most challenging aspects of working for ourselves

- Coping with the growth of the business and also all those unexplained mini catastrophes that occur that you cannot plan for: floods, staff leaving, production runs being late, etc.
- We really have tried to learn from all our mistakes or misjudgements and try not to act or remark too quickly. We are not as hot headed as we once were. We see it as a series of problems and we have to find a way to solve them to keep as many people happy as possible.
- People are the most challenging aspect of our business, whether it be clients, staff or suppliers.

Our scariest moment

We have had so many scary moments no one particular time stands out from another. I don't know if it is the same for other small businesses but we have had people lie to us, steal from us, try to sue us for all manner of things, it can be heartbreaking at times and it does make you tougher everytime something new comes along to deal with. But we understand now that it is all part of business. There comes a time when you have to remove yourself from the situation and deal with it as a business owner and not allow your own feelings to come in to it.

Being women and having children and homes to run as well as having a business you work at full time is very demanding. Your own health and problems can't come into it.

We have tried to treat all our staff very well over the years but there is no way of knowing how someone will react when you have to let them go or when you discover they have been acting inappropriately.

You just have to be prepared for anything. Our walls at Lello are filled with inspirational statements and to us it is all about never giving up. Each new day brings new challenges and somehow to survive you have to deal with them as best you can.

Our advice

- Be prepared for anything. You have to be extremely resilient and put in 110 per cent. You can't be precious about what you do and you can't know everything.
- You have to value and praise those who work with you as they will help you get to where you want to be.
- You have to have a plan B up your sleeve in any situation and you can never, ever give up.
- You have to enjoy the journey. There is no point in waiting for the day you might make your fortune or what might be.

Sometimes the fortune is in the journey you take to wherever you are going.

- You have to try and make the most out of every day no matter how bad it is. Tomorrow is always a new day.
- You have to learn to carry on with your life and your family no matter what.
- The home/work balance is all about organization. Work will have to take over at times, but you can't take it home with you. I leave my work at the front door and when I walk in the house I am someone's wife and mother to my children.
- We have been lucky and always taken account of childcare within the company. It has worked for us and allowed us to see our children at all times. It's a tall order, but you have to put as much effort and time into your home life and your marriage as you do your business. I think it is exceptionally hard for women.

Our strategies

- Having onsite childcare at the office – a fully fledged nursery with nannies employed by the business.
- Planning school events long in advance to make sure they don't conflict with work commitments.
- Having a very supportive husband.
- Making time with the children very special.
- In many circumstances being able to plan meetings so that they allow us to drop the children off first. Many of our clients have children and are more than happy to see us late morning.
- Recognize that there are some things you can't get round.
- Being extremely organized and being able to ask for help.

Making It Happen for You – Determination

What did Fiona and Karen do?

- Turned rejection and failure from a negative to a positive and didn't take failure personally.
- Kept focusing on future success.
- Listened to their encouraging inner voice.

How can you model Fiona and Karen and be determined?

- Begin with the end in mind and keep focusing on it.
- Turn feedback into feedforward.
- Use your inner voice to support you.

How determined are you?

Think about what you want to achieve in your business. With that in mind, score yourself from 0 to 10 on the statements below. A score of 0 means you really disagree and a score of 10 means you really agree.

- If I fail at something I don't tend to take it personally.
- When things go wrong I just get back up and try again.
- I tend to keep going with things.
- When things go wrong, I think about how I can make them different next time.
- When things go wrong I try to find a way forward rather than looking for people to blame.
- People often comment on my tenacity.
- I am always very focused on what I am trying to achieve.
- I find that the voice in my head encourages me to keep going.

- I have a 'can-do' attitude.
- Other people often say to me if anyone can do it, you can do it.

CHECK YOUR ATTITUDE

Add up your total score out of 100.

- *If you scored 85–100 points* – You're a very determined individual. Use the exercises below to be absolutely sure you're not missing any other opportunities to be even more determined.
- *If you scored 50–84 points* – You can be determined, but might wobble a bit at times. Make yourself as determined as dynamite by trying out the explosive exercises below.
- *If you scored 0–49 points* – You may find that you lose heart easily. Set your determination dynamo spinning and get some momentum by trying out the strategies below.

Three Steps to Becoming More Determined

STEP 1: FOCUS ON WHAT YOU WANT

We've all seen that child in the supermarket, the one who's having the most almighty tantrum. They know what they want and they won't stop until they get it. They have an unwavering focus on what they desire, and whether it's a bar of chocolate or a bag of crisps, every person within earshot knows too. This unwavering determination and focus on the end game very often reap reward, as the browbeaten mother grudgingly gives in and the child's determination wins out. Our determination is an in-built survival mechanism and partly what makes it work is having something to be determined about.

Many surviving Jewish prisoners of war, kept in horrific camps during the Second World War, testify to the power of determination. Often the only thing to keep them going was the vision in their minds that one day they would be free. With something to aim for or to focus on, we are more able to find the will and determination within ourselves to get there. The best dieters not only have a goal but a vision of the end game, often putting pictures of their slimmer ideal selves on the fridge. When they see this, it strengthens their resolve and determination to succeed. Similarly, Fiona and Karen realized that 'businesses fail when they give up'. You can do the same, by checking in with your goals and dreams each day so it ignites your determination.

Exercise: Check in with your future

Once a day, check in and reconnect with your dream or your goal, to remind yourself why you are doing all the hard work and taking the steps you are. Sit in a quiet place and look out into your future. Think of and focus on a point in your future when your dream has been realized and your goal has been met. As you look at that future, see yourself there in this place of success. Notice how it makes you feel. Does it make you feel more determined? Look at that future 'you' and ask if that 'you' of the future can give you any advice about how she managed to achieve her goal. Let that advice give you an injection of determination.

STEP 2: TURN FEEDBACK INTO FEEDFORWARD

Many times in Lello's story there were setbacks, but what clearly stands out is the way in which those setbacks were dealt with. Never were disasters or failures seen in a negative way. Never were they internalized or blame assigned. Instead, they were viewed as part of the learning curve in setting up a business and turned into learning opportunities, rather then events to be commiserated about and moped over. Failure was reframed as a positive thing, feedback.

Exercise: Feedforward

Think about something that has gone wrong in your life at some time in the past. Turn this episode into a learning experience by asking yourself the following questions:

- What can I learn from this?
- If this happened again, what would I do differently?
- What good can come of this?
- How can I use this learning in other parts of my life?
- What can I do to stop this happening again?

STEP 3: USE YOUR INNER VOICE TO SUPPORT YOU

Your inner voice can help keep you determined or it can encourage you to give up. I always think that children must have wonderfully encouraging inner voices. Think about all those things we learnt as children that required a bucket full of determination. How about learning to walk? You probably don't remember doing it yourself, but no doubt you've seen a small child attempting to take their first steps. Very rarely do babies go from crawling to walking in one go. Instead, they make various attempts with differing degrees of success to get up and roam around on two feet. Inevitably they fall over a number of times in the process. Do you think for one moment there's a voice in that baby's head saying 'You've failed' every time she falls over? I very much doubt it. I believe there's a voice in there coaching her and encouraging her to get up and have another go.

Have you noticed that babies are usually surrounded by a group of adoring adults, who also see the falling over not as a failure to walk but as a step in the right direction on the path of learning to walk? These adults are encouraging and results focused. They don't see failing as a problem. What they see is a child who is learning to walk, rather than a child who keeps falling over.

Take lessons from the baby and tune into your inner voice. Let it help and encourage you. All too often we let our internal voice beat us up. Is your inner voice solution focused or is it blame and problem focused? If it's the latter, change the record. Start focusing on solutions and learning.

'Lello would rather employ the right person to do the job and make the working hours fit, rather than the other way round,' says Fiona. Talking to yourself positively and providing yourself with feedforward will fuel your determination.

Exercise: Turn down the volume

Blame, retribution and guilt fuel the fire of perceived failure and hold you where you are. If your inner voice isn't being terribly supporting, why not try turning down the volume?

- Identify where the voice in your head that diminishes your determination comes from. Is it the front, the back, the left or the right? Is it inside or outside your head? Are you being seduced in stereo or just in one ear?
- Acknowledge the voice. Recognize that it is trying to help you by protecting you from failure.
- Imagine you have a volume control on the side of your head.
- Using the control knob in your mind, turn down the voice that you don't want to listen to. Make a choice to listen only to the voices of inner influence that support you and help to keep you determined.
- If only it was so easy to do this with other people's voices!

Now all that remains is for you to make a date with the business destiny of your dreams, divvy up some determination and get yourself there.

'To follow without halt, one aim: There's the secret of success.'
                                                    Anna Pavlova

Enthusiasm

Enthusiasm is infectious. What attitude do you choose to spread?

Enthusiasm in any form is very attractive. Allison and I were at the One Life Exhibition at Earls Court, sponsored by the Virgin One Account. There were motivational speakers and workshops as part of the day. One of the speakers asked the audience, 'How are you?' There were a lot of mumbles and two enthusiastic replies of 'Brilliant'. No prizes for guessing who from! At the end of the workshop the presenter came over to us for a chat because of our enthusiasm.

Mentoring Moments

I was asked to help Wendy Millington of Average Joes, an all-male grooming salon, with marketing her new business. Wendy attended one of my workshops and I was struck by her amazing enthusiasm – not only for what she does, but also how she can help others. Wendy is a savvy businesswoman who has lived in the Caribbean and the UK and there isn't much she doesn't know about marketing. However, she still felt she may learn something from the workshop. It turned out that the main benefit for Wendy were the connections she made and Wendy became an avid member of our Business Buddies networking events too. Other people in the workshop gained tremendously from Wendy's experience, passion and overall enthusiasm for life.

Entrepreneur's Experience

A removal company had asked for help to upskill its workforce, particularly in view of the many Brits relocating to Spain. The owner wanted to ensure that his workforce was equipped to compete. We developed a particularly good rapport and I asked him to share with me how he addressed his marketing for his business to expand so rapidly.

His secret is simple. He believes, as I do, that the best form of advertising is recommendation. He recognizes that moving house, particularly a relocation abroad, is a very stressful time and anything he can do to take away any stress must be a bonus. The day after the customer moves in he sends a huge bouquet of flowers, wrapped in cellophane with their own water (no need to find a vase). Attached to the flowers is a 'Welcome to your new home' greeting, along with a batch of cards with the customer's contact details to give to relatives, friends and business colleagues. On the back of the cards are his company's logo and contact details. End result – the customer is not just satisfied but delighted and the remover's contact details have gone automatically to all the customer's contacts. He spreads the word beautifully.

How are you going to be different from your competitors and spread the enthusiasm through your marketing? Think about how you talk about your business. Know what you do well, what makes you different to everyone else and how you can put it across to someone in the most simple, succinct way possible. Always think about how what you produce or the service you provide benefits your customer and when you are selling it, sell the benefits.

Making It – Meeting Lynne Franks, SEED

Knocking at the shiny painted front door of Lynne Franks' Maida Vale home, I felt quite nervous about meeting her. Her reputation goes before her. If I were to believe what I had read in the media, then I was about to meet a New Age woman, rumoured to be the inspiration behind the character of Edina from the hit comedy series *Absolutely Fabulous*, who now spends her time hugging trees!

Walking up the stairs to Lynne's flat, I notice that her home is adorned with beautiful artefacts from all over the world. She invites me to sit at the kitchen table where we share a two-hour chat over numerous cups of herbal tea. As I talk to the real Lynne I make my mind up to never believe what I read in the papers. Lynne is clearly an experienced, savvy, grounded businesswoman, with a huge amount of wisdom that she is willing to share with others. I have never quite understood the value of academics with no commercial experience teaching business skills. There is a depth of experience that comes with having been there and 'done it' for real that academia can't convey. It reminds me of a childless health visitor teaching new mothers how to look after their babies when they have no experience of being a mum themselves. We don't all have the time or energy to learn by our own mistakes, so listening and learning from people who have 'been there, done it and worn the t-shirt' seems a winning idea to me.

Lynne began what became the UK's leading public relations consultancy
when she was only 21, working from her kitchen table. She was hugely
successful in the 1980s and 1990s, making London Fashion Week
and Swatch watches household names. She sold her London-based
agency in 1992. This coincided with the end of her marriage and was
prompted by the death of two close friends from cancer and a realiza-
tion that she wanted a better quality of life. Lynne knew that there had
to be a better way of working and living so she could feel fulfilled on
a personal and business level. She dropped out of the working world
to give herself the time and space to discover who she really was and
what she really wanted. Gone were the manic days of juggling life
as owner of a fast-paced PR business and working mum, but making
so many major changes at the same time is something she certainly
doesn't recommend!

Some years later, a changed person, Lynne created the What Women
Want festival in London, featuring Sinead O'Connor, Chrissie Hynde
and Germaine Greer. Prior to attending the United Nations' Women's
Conference in Beijing, she also spearheaded the launch of the UK's first
women's radio station. These events gave her many insights into what
she saw as the beginning of the twenty-first century's feminization of
society. She went on to write successful books *The SEED Handbook*,
The SEED Manifesto and *GROW: The Modern Woman's Handbook* and
developed the SEED training course, which shows a holistic way for
women to begin and grow their business through workshops, coaching and networking. SEED is currently being delivered as a training
programme throughout the UK.

I asked Lynne what she thinks is really important for women. 'We
know the thing that holds women back is self-confidence and self-
esteem, but I think it's about believing in yourself,' she said. 'You can't

get anywhere until you do, so we do a little bit of work on ourselves before we can even start on actually changing our life. Whether that's personal or professional, at any level we really have to be in touch with who we are. That's the first thing, acknowledging who you really are not who you have become, because that is living by your parents' and your teachers' values and opinions. I think for many women that's being in touch with the feminine side.

'The women I meet and work with usually fall into three categories. First are the ones who haven't had kids, who have concentrated on their careers up to the age of 40 and living in their male energy. They get to 35 and they start getting sick. They have got confidence, they are out there working in large corporations in roles such as accountants, lawyers and engineers, but they aren't living by their own values. They need to realize it's OK to live by feminine values and to value those values. They need to be told it's OK to be a woman.

'Then you have got women who have perhaps given up what they were doing to have children and now want to start doing something again based around what they believe in. Although they've kept working, their priority is with the kids, at home doing the stuff around the house, looking after their man and all the rest of it. OK, they have children, but really don't want to disappear into a complete mess of nappies. They'd like to be themselves and value themselves again, do something which helps other women as well as giving them back their self-esteem.

'Then there's a third group of women who are 45 plus. The children have left home, they are ready to do something for themselves. The older women particularly tend to have the lowest self-esteem, they are probably on their own and not expecting to be. They have lost their sense of self, of purpose. For everyone the common theme is about leading a fulfilled life and finding out who they really are.

'My working life began at the age of 12, working in my father's butchers shop. At school I was hopeless. I could never be bothered to do any studying of any description, but I was the form captain. I'm sure it was because I was so bossy and a born organizer. I was always organizing the school social dances. I also loved to read and talk and do public speaking and being centre stage. I left school at 16, mainly because I hated being told what to do. I was generally a bit of a rebel. I landed my first job at a solicitor's office, typing out the intimate details of people's divorces. I enjoyed the money I earned and spent it on the latest fashions. I was a typical London 1960s mod with a Vidal Sassoon symmetrical hairdo, dressed in a Biba dress and matching scarf.

'I gradually gained confidence in the workplace and left the safety of my typist job and began temping for an advertising agency. I felt that I had arrived, as there were lots of fashionable people there who I admired. I was soon transferred to the PR department, ironically without even knowing what PR was! I soon began to get involved with promoting products to the public and the press. I stayed for about a year, then moving to the prestigious and trendy *Petticoat* magazine, the UK's first teenage girls' mag. Eve Pollard interviewed me for the position of secretary. She took me on and encouraged me to help her on photo shoots and to start writing little pieces of my own. I soon found myself promoted to writing a regular page about London in the 'swinging sixties'. I worked alongside the most seriously trendy person I had ever met, Janet Street Porter. She was bold and intimidating yet very kind. By day I spent my time at previews and launches, by night I went to trendy clubs with my boyfriend. Trouble was, I was so exhausted with the endless stream of partying that I was always turning up late for work. The editor decided that my personality was more suited to a PR role and politely let me know that my services were no longer required.

'I continued with journalism and worked for about two years for Freemans' mail order catalogue. It was here that I learnt the craft of writing and editing, but my social life took its toll on the job again, which I had also begun to find tedious. I moved to a temporary stint with a PR guy and worked with enormous enthusiasm on London Fashion Week. It was here that a fascinating person approached me dressed in a brown lurex suit, Katherine Hamnett. She and her partner Ann Buck soon became my friends and she suggested I began my own PR company. She was to be my first client and paid me £20 a week. That was how my business began at the age of 21 from my kitchen table.

'I had passion in my ideas. I really believed in what I was doing, working for fashion designers, I believed in their designs. I suppose I had a genuine enthusiasm for life, whether it be fashion or helping people, I just really enjoyed what I did. I was single-minded, which is a very male attribute. I also had a good business role model in my grandmother. She had her own business when she was 18. She had started another business when she was married and when her husband got sick she took over the family business. I'd seen what she was able to do and I think almost subconsciously learnt from it.

'The business grew at a fast and furious rate and in the first nine years of owning it I had got married, had both my daughter and son, and my husband had come to work alongside me and the other 15 or so staff. I still remained single-minded and put the business first and my family second. By the age of 30 I owned the UK's best-known PR agency, but at what cost? As for my attitude, what changed me was the pace of life I was leading. I found it increasingly difficult to maintain, I also started to get sick. Time was my biggest enemy. To the outside world I had everything – a flourishing, profitable, high-profile business, a husband who I worked with so we spent lots of time together, two beautiful children, a lovely home. All the trappings of success compared to the outside world's values. To me, this never seemed enough. It was as if something was missing.

'I began to feel awful, really ill. I was always running on adrenalin and was filling my body with caffeine and sugary snacks on the run, always chasing the next piece of business. I was under an enormous amount of stress. Public relations is an all-consuming career and I was doing too much juggling, throwing things up into the air and rushing to catch them, sometimes not catching them quickly enough. I was putting my business first and spending very little time with my children. They were looked after by an endless stream of nannies. I was hardly ever at home. The only conversations I had with my husband were about work and the passion evaporated. I had reached the point where I was realizing that business success, money and possessions did not necessarily make me happy. The inevitable accompanying stress, lack of quality time with my family and friends and always living in the future created an emptiness and lack of centre that was destroying me. I asked myself "Can I have it all?" and the fact was I couldn't, something had to give. I also lost two very dear friends to cancer and realized that I needed to stop, take stock, examine my life and make changes for me to feel good and calm.

'I made the decision to sell my business with an option to work as an employee within it, and was still working in it when I began to look for the tools to help me feel well. It was this quest to feel better that led me to alternative ways of healing. I began to use my intuitive sense and things started to fall into place. I confronted my husband Paul, as I had suspected he was having an affair and I was right. For ten years Paul and I were brilliant work partners, not brilliant life partners. I am a strong woman and that made him feel threatened; when a man feels threatened, the only way he can actually really feel better about himself is to knock away at your foundations. Because I was so fragile and my self-esteem wasn't high, it didn't take much. I remember feeling a great sense of relief, as I finally felt justified in getting out of a marriage that I no longer felt happy in.

'Once that decision was made, leaving Lynne Franks PR was easy. I was letting go and although the pain was great, I knew it was the right thing to do. So in one week I let go of everything I used to think mattered – material wealth, a long marriage, a high profile and a successful career. I needed to "find myself" and make friends with my children, who were now teenagers and I was regretting the time I had lost with them. I am pleased to say that I am now very close to both of them.

'I spent the next few years travelling and experiencing a peaceful existence, working with alternative healers and learning to be myself. Being yourself is a much more comforting place to be and this "space" I created for myself led to me developing SEED, which stands for Sustainable Enterprise Empowerment Dynamics. This comes from a passion for the empowerment of women through economic independence, based on spiritual and values-led principles. I've learnt that it's about getting things into perspective. The first rule of life for any woman is to be true to yourself, know who you are, get in touch with who you are, value, love and be yourself. That's what I've been learning to do. Even though I had all that big success, I was still lacking self-esteem in certain areas of my life. Giving up my career and saying goodbye to my marriage was hard to do all at the same time, but I knew it was right. I am now learning to appreciate myself. The idea of my work is to give women tools so they don't have to wait until they are 55 like me.

'Life is a journey and we learn by our mistakes, but I think we need to accelerate that learning process right now, because I believe that the future of the world is in the hands of the women. I do believe in a divine presence, that I call God, and who is to say God isn't a woman? I think that the old way of doing things, which is not anti-men but the old system, is destructive and is based on power and greed, which is why we've got terrible things happening all over the world, and it is women that are building the bridges from community to community. Within our own world we have to create the bridges, create these scenarios and opportunities for women to get together and talk about their lives. That's what my life is now, committed to creating opportunities for bridges to be built, to share everything that I have learnt, to give back to help many people. I'm one of the army of "female warriors", working towards creating a new world, a world of feminine leadership alongside men that's very community led. I don't want to die knowing that I didn't do my utmost to give my gifts back, because I do have a wonderful life. I've got incredible friends and a loving close family. I have a fabulous life now that I live it in a holistic, harmonious way.'

I was curious to find out more about the feminine way to do business that Lynne champions so enthusiastically through the SEED programme. She told me that in this way of doing business you begin by examining your own life to ensure that you are creating and sustaining your business in a way that suits you and your lifestyle. It's also important at this point to define your own version of success clearly. SEED is about the passions that you have in life and ensuring that you work using your passions and talents in the best way possible, so that ultimately you can create a future for yourself and family where you are happy doing what you are doing.

The SEED book and learning programme intrigued me and I decided to join in a one-day SEED experience at the Amadeus Centre in Maida Vale to see what I thought. The day began with Lynne giving a talk about her work and her reasons for doing it. She bubbled over with enthusiasm and passion for helping others to achieve what they wanted in life. At the end of a day filled with inspiring talks, nutrition advice, singing, soul searching, creating and sharing, I knew that SEED was something I wanted to be part of. I entered into the SEED philosophy, took a full programme and began gardening! As recommended by the SEED course instructors, I cleared out my clutter, I planted the seeds of my vision, I organized my tool shed, I addressed my finances, I began to create my SEED community, sketched my garden plan and with the fabulous people I have met enjoyed numerous garden parties. I have experienced first hand that there is in fact a revolution going on in the world and it is coming from the grass roots. It's a revolution of sustainable entrepreneurs, mainly women, and it's about personal growth as well as an economic tool. (Franks, 2005)

Lynne speaks and interviews entrepreneurs at conferences all over the world and her enthusiasm is infectious. She has learnt to stop and reflect when things get too mad. She chooses to not allow herself to be under too much pressure: she works to her strengths and delegates the rest. Lynne asks you to remember one thing: 'No one is perfect, but I'm doing the best I can.'

Lynne's business is now moving into a new stage of sustainable growth and has seen the following changes over the past months:

- Knowing that everything I believe in about women moving into their power as leaders in business and community is coming about and that we are getting to a tipping point.
- Recognition and launch of the SEED Women Into Enterprise Blended Learning Programme, the only national modular women's business course.

- The first group of women accredited as SEED Coaches in our new coaching programme. Plus so many other things, including the start of building a SEEDWorks business centre.

Lynne's way of finding time for herself

- Get up early in the morning and stay balanced with my schedule.
- Live and work in the country for several days a week where I don't have lots of meetings.
- Exercise first thing in the morning and find time for meditation.
- Take my puppy out for lots of walks every day.

Lynne's advice to women entrepreneurs

- Discuss it with your family first.
- Make sure you can pay your mortgage or rent. Make sure the sums work.
- Be passionate about your business.
- Do your research.
- Talk to as many people as you can about your new ideas to get their feedback.
- Follow the SEED Manifesto by Lynne Franks to create your business the *feminine way*:

I, ..., affirm that I will
constantly plant seeds as well as pick the blooms

***

Make the space and time to stay in tune with my higher self

***

Never let go of the big vision

***

Put my values, including integrity, compassion, and love at the
centre of my enterprise

* * *

Remember the three Rs: respect for self, respect for others,
responsibility for all my actions

* * *

Believe in myself so others will too

* * *

Keep humour and laughter as vital ingredients
of my business plan

* * *

Get up early in the morning

* * *

Not neglect my personal relationships, loved ones and friends
in any way

* * *

Manifest abundance in all areas of my life

* * *

Keep my clutter to a minimum

* * *

Recognize my gifts and delegate the rest

* * *

Look at difficult situations from all perspectives

* * *

Welcome in mentors and mentor others in return

* * *

Light candles every day and surround myself with fresh flowers

* * *

Give people more than they expect

* * *

Talk slowly but think quickly

***

When I lose, I don't lose the lesson

***

Know my industry

***

Keep improving my technology skills

***

Smile when picking up the phone

***

Remember my body is my most important tool – stretch, exercise, breathe, go for a walk, dance

***

Every day try and read a poem, listen to an inspiring piece of music, look at a wonderful painting or go into nature

***

Drink six to eight glasses of pure water every day

***

Listen as well as talk

***

Learn the rules, and then break some

***

Know there is nothing more sexy than confidence

***

Remember that no one, not even myself is perfect, but I'm doing the best I can

SIGNED ....

Date ....

Source: Franks (2005)

Lynne says that her biggest inspiration to start her enterprise was 'every woman I knew or met' and other influences included Dadi Janki, leader of the women-led spiritual organization the Brahma Kumaris, and Anita Roddick. She defines the word 'success' for herself as 'still feeling so passionate about SEED: knowing that I've helped so many women from so many different backgrounds help themselves' and is kept motivated by 'my own creativity and endless ideas, plus the women that I work with'.

Making It Happen for You – Enthusiasm

What did Lynne do?

- Chose to feel enthusiastic.
- Looked enthusiastic.
- Sounded enthusiastic.

How can you model Lynne and be enthusiastic?

- Choose your state of mind and feel enthusiastic.
- Learn how to look enthusiastic.
- Speak the language of enthusiasm.

How enthusiastic are you?

Think about how you come across as a businesswoman. With that in mind, score yourself from 0 to 10 on the statements below. A score of 0 means you really disagree and a score of 10 means you really agree:

- I tend to get very excited about what I am trying to achieve.
- When I talk to others they tend to get excited about what I am talking about.

- I tend to be enthusiastic most of the time.
- I am enthusiastic about other people and their ideas, not just my own.
- People often find me inspirational.
- When asked about an enjoyable event in my life, for example a holiday, I wax lyrical about it.
- I use lots of gestures when I speak.
- I sound enthusiastic when I speak.
- When I talk I feel enthusiasm in my body.
- I am fast paced.

CHECK YOUR ATTITUDE

Add up your total score out of 100.

- *If you scored 85–100 points* – You are an enthusiastic soul, quite possibly contagiously so. Use the following techniques to help you switch it on and turn it up when you really need it to reel in other people who can help you to achieve your goals.
- *If you scored 50–84 points* – Your enthusiasm probably ebbs and flows like the tide. Read and practise the following exercises so you have it at your beck and call. Make your enthusiasm the servant of which you are master.
- *If you scored 0–49 points* – You need to get some enthusiasm flowing through your body if you want to have it oozing out your pores. Get working on the exercises.

Three Steps to Being Enthusiastic

Certain people just ooze enthusiasm. When you're in their presence the enthusiasm they exhibit is catching. Like a bad case of conjunctivitis or a bout of flu, whether you want it or not, when you come into contact with a carrier you find you've got it too. Lynne personifies enthusiasm and because it is so contagious, you too become enthusiastic about whatever she's saying. How do you transform yourself into a carrier and transmitter of the only virus everybody wants to catch, enthusiasm?

To communicate an emotion to others you have to feel it in your own body. It's not very easy to transmit enthusiasm if the emotion you're feeling is sadness, distress or anger. To show enthusiasm you've got to feel it. You need the ability to access a feeling of enthusiasm whenever you want it.

STEP 1: GET AN ENTHUSIASTIC STATE OF MIND

It isn't necessarily appropriate to be enthusiastic every minute of the day. For example, nobody is going to thank you for being overenthusiastic at Great Aunt Maud's funeral. However, it is great to have an awareness of when you want to be enthusiastic and when it might be helpful. A little dollop of contagious enthusiasm when you're talking to the bank manager might come in handy. Like any emotion you have experienced, if you've done it once you can do it again. Like a light switch, you can turn it on and off at your leisure. When you need to exude enthusiasm, here's how you can access that emotional state instantly. And create your own enthusiasm 'on' switch.

Exercise: Switch your enthusiasm on

Find yourself a quiet place to practise this technique.

1. Think of an opportunity or situation when you want to feel enthusiastic, but right now when you think about this impending event you feel anything but.

2. Recall a time from your past when you felt really enthusiastic.

3. As vividly as you can, remember that time. As you recall it in your mind's eye notice all the *sounds*, all the *sights* and all the *feelings* from that time that you strongly associate with this memory of enthusiasm. Really concentrate on experiencing this as intensely as you can. (Some people find it helpful to close their eyes when doing this visualization.)

4. Stop concentrating and shake yourself gently to break the feeling.

5. Think about something that you could use to trigger the enthusiastic feeling that will act like your 'on' switch. Clenching your fist or squeezing your thumb and forefinger together are possibilities, but choose something that works for you.

6. Once again in your mind revisit the experience of enthusiasm that you identified earlier, as intensely as you can. As the feeling seems at its most intense, 'fire' the trigger that's going to act as your 'on' switch. Then stop concentrating on the memory and shake yourself gently to break the feeling. Do this ten times.

7. Test to see if the trigger works by recalling the future situation in which you want to feel enthusiastic. As you think about the coming event, use your trigger to switch on your enthusiasm. The feeling should come instantly. If it doesn't, repeat firing the trigger until you do feel enthusiastic when you think of the future situation.

8. Using your new-found trigger, switch on enthusiasm whenever you need it.

In this case the emotional state you are creating is enthusiasm, but this is a generic tool and you can use it to develop 'on' and 'off' switches for any emotional state you want to experience.

STEP 2: LOOK ENTHUSIASTIC

For your enthusiasm to come across, you need to look authentically enthusiastic. In communication the majority of our message comes from how we look, not what we say. How enthusiastic do you look?

Exercise: Modelling enthusiasm

Watch television personalities being interviewed. Notice what those who convey enthusiasm actually do. What kind of gestures do they use? How do they hold themselves? What is their posture like? What is it about them that makes them look enthusiastic? Begin to model this behaviour. Try it on for size. Think of one person you admire and find enthusiastic. Practise acting like them and try behaving with their enthusiasm. See if it suits you.

STEP 3: SPEAK THE LANGUAGE OF ENTHUSIASM

What you look like is key, but what you sound like is also of great importance when conveying a message. If you want to appear enthusiastic you have to sound enthusiastic. Enthusiasm is transmitted in your tone of voice and will affect your listener's internal state and level of interest. Lynne often uses language that you would associate with an enthusiastic person. She speaks many strong words that get over her sense of enthusiasm to anyone listening. These words in turn evoke an enthusiastic reaction in the listener.

Notice what kind of words you are using when you talk to other people about your ideas. Are they downbeat or upbeat? Do they give what you're saying an injection of enthusiasm? A really good everyday example of this is the way you greet people. When you shake hands with a new customer and they ask you how you are, what do you say? Do you say

'I'm great' or 'I'm not bad'? Both are acceptable answers, but one will undoubtedly make the speaker sound more enthusiastic about life.

In Lynne's interview she often describes things using upbeat, affirming words that help to convey her enthusiasm for what she does. The lefthand side in the table shows some of Lynne's words. The righthand side shows the sentiment of what she said. One sounds more enthusiastic than the other because of the words that are used.

Enthusiastic	Not so enthusiastic
We need to accelerate that learning process *right* now.	We need to accelerate that learning process now.
I *really* believed in what I was doing	I believed in what I was doing.

Exercise: Wash away woolly words

Find someone who is willing to do a bit of an experiment with you. On a dictaphone or a personal tape player, tape your voice having a normal conversation with your partner. In this conversation, sound enthusiastic. Play this back and focus on the types of words you use. Do you use words that convey enthusiasm? Or do you just get over the basic points so the person receiving your message gets information but not enthusiasm? Are your voice pattern and pitch interesting or monotone? If you were listening to you, would you believe that you were an enthusiastic type of person? If not, what needs to change? Use the tape recorder to experiment with some different approaches.

If you want to spread enthusiasm as easily as strawberry jam, you've got to look, sound and say it with enthusiasm. When people get enthusiastic about you, who knows where it might lead.

'*Enthusiasm is the yeast that makes your hopes shine to the stars. Enthusiasm is the sparkle in your eyes, the swing in your gait, the grip of your hand, the irresistible surge of will and energy to execute your ideas.*'

Henry Ford

Epilogue

We sincerely hope you have been inspired by the stories we have shared with you. Whether you start your business or not, have boundaries in your life. Know what you will and won't accept. Have you read 'Desiderata'? We love this poem, along with 'When I am an old woman I shall wear purple' by Jenny Joseph.

Here is our version of 'Desiderata'. There are little stories behind it that make us smile. Have a go at writing your own, if only to make you smile…

OUR DESIDERATA

Instead of waiting to be old to wear purple, wear it now – the brighter the better.

Remember, if you are a mumpreneur it is your duty and your right to embarrass your children.

Dance like no one's watching – always end in the splits.

Make laughter a part of your business.

Use your head and your heart in equal measures when making big decisions.

When creating a business event, give more than your customers expect and leave them wanting more – turn it into a show.

When you blag, blag it big.

Treat yourself as you would want others to treat you.

Always wear a good bra – you never know when you will want to wear it à la French and Saunders, on top of your clothes.

Rules are made to be broken – but don't break the law.

When organizing a tête-à-tête, do it en laugh!

May you wear your life with ease and grace.

Be true to yourself and enjoy!

Remember, it's all about attitude. Choose your attitude wisely.

Wishing you our very best

Lou & Allison

Recommended reading

Allen, Paul (2007) *Your Ethical Business: How to Plan, Start and Succeed in a Company with a Conscience*, ngo.media.

Ashton, Robert (2004) *The Entrepreneur's Book of Checklists: 1000 Tips to Help You Start and Grow Your Business*, Prentice Hall.

Bannatyne, Duncan (2006) *Anyone Can Do It: My Story*, Orion.

Barrow, Colin (2004) *Starting a Business For Dummies*, John Wiley & Sons Ltd.

Black, A&C (2006) *Good Small Business Guide: How to Start and Grow Your Own Business*, A&C Black.

Borg, James (2004) *Persuasion: The Art of Influencing People*, Prentice Hall.

Branson, Sir Richard (2005) *Losing My Virginity: The Autobiography*, Virgin Books.

Branson, Sir Richard (2006) *Screw It, Let's Do It: Lessons in Life*, Virgin Books.

Branson, Sir Richard and Barrow, Paul (2005) *The Best-Laid Business Plans: How to Write Them, How to Pitch Them*, Virgin Books.

Bridge, Rachel (2004) *How I Made It: 40 Successful Entrepreneurs Reveal All*, Kogan Page.

Bridge, Rachel (2006) *My Big Idea: 30 Successful Entrepreneurs Reveal How They Found Inspiration*, Kogan Page.

Browning, Robert (2003) *Setting Up and Running a Limited Company: A Comprehensive Guide to Forming and Operating a Company as a Director and Shareholder*, How To Books.

Clark, Val (2005) *Start and Run Your Own Shop: How to Open a Successful Retail Business (Small Business Start Ups)*, How To Books.

Dewberry, Michelle (2007) *Anything Is Possible*, Orion.

Dilts, Robert B. (1990) *Changing Belief Systems with Neuro-Linguistic Programming*, Meta Publications.

Dilts, Robert and De Lozier, Judith (2000) *Encyclopedia of Systemic NLP and NLP New Coding*, NLP University Press.

Elliott, Mark S. (2006) *How to Run a Successful Pub: A Comprehensive Guide to Acquiring and Running Your Own Licensed Premises*, How To Books.

Fox, Scott (2006) *Internet Riches: The Simple Money-Making Secrets of Online Millionaires*, Amacom.

Franks, Lynne (2005) *The SEED Handbook: The Feminine Way to Create Business*, Hay House.

Gerber, Michael E. (1994) *The E-Myth Revisited*, HarperCollins.

Gilbert, Andy (2005) *Go MAD®: The Art of Making A Difference*, Go MAD® Books.

Hashemi, Sahar and Hashemi, Bobby (2003) *Anyone Can Do It: Building Coffee Republic From Our Kitchen Table: 57 Real Life Laws on Entrepreneurship*, Capstone.

Hingston, Peter (2004) *The Best Small Business Accounts Book (Blue Version): For a Non-VAT Registered Small Business*, Hingston Publishing Co.

Horovitz, Jacques and Ohlsson-Corboz, Anne-Valerie (2007) *A Dream with a Deadline: How to Turn a Vision for Tomorrow into a Plan for Today*, Financial Times/Prentice Hall.

Kawasaki, Guy (2004) *The Art of the Start: The Time-Tested and Battle-Hardened Guide for Anyone Starting Anything*, Portfolio.

Kimball, Cheryl (2006) *Start Your Florist Shop and Other Floral Businesses*, Entrepreneur Press.

Knight, Peter (2004) *The Highly Effective Marketing Plan: A Proven, Practical, Planning Process for Companies of All Sizes*, Prentice Hall.

Le Marinel, Alan (2004) *Start and Run Your Own Business: The Complete Guide to Setting Up and Managing a Small Business*, How To Books.

Livingston, Jessica (2007) *Founders at Work: Stories of Startups' Early Days*, APRESS.

Martin, Lucy and Mehta, Bella (2006) *Make It Your Business: The Ultimate Business Start-up Guide for Women*, How To Books.

Matthews, Dan and Collier, Marsha (2006) *Starting a Business on eBay.co.uk For Dummies,* UK Edition, John Wiley & Sons Ltd.

Miller, Stephen (2002) *Starting and Running a Sandwich-Coffee Bar: An Insider Guide (Successful Business Start-ups),* How To Books.

Mitchell, Allison (2006) *Time Management for Manic Mums,* Hay House.

Mohr, Angie (2005) *Start and Run a Bookkeeping Business (Start and Run a Business),* How To Books.

Mullins, John (2006) *The New Business Road Test: What Entrepreneurs and Executives Should Do Before Writing a Business Plan,* Financial Times/ Prentice Hall.

Ready, Romilla and Burton, Kate (2004) *Neuro-linguistic Programming for Dummies,* John Wiley & Sons.

Parker, Ken (2007) *How to Buy and Run a Small Hotel: The Complete Guide to Setting Up and Managing Your Own Hotel, Guesthouse or B & B,* How To Books.

Parks, Steve (2004) *Start Your Business: Week by Week,* Prentice Hall.

Parks, Steve (2006) *How to be an Entrepreneur: The Six Secrets of Self-Made Success,* Prentice Hall.

Parks, Steve (2006) *Small Business Handbook,* Prentice Hall.

Peck, Alan (2005) *Buying and Running a Florist Shop,* Alan Peck Publishing.

Posen, Zac and Gehlhar, Mary (2005) *The Fashion Designers Survival Guide: An Insiders Look at Starting and Running Your Own Fashion Business,* Kaplan Business.

Power, Paul (2007) *How to Start Your Own Gardening Business: An Insider Guide to Setting Yourself Up as a Professional Gardener,* How To Books.

Rickertsen, Rick (2001) *Buyout: The Insiders Guide to Buying Your Own Company,* Amacom.

Rickman, Cheryl D. and Roddick, Dame Anita (2005) *The Small Business Start-Up Guide to Starting the Business You've Dreamed Of,* How To Books.

Ridderstrale, Jonas and Nordstrom, Kjell (2001) *Funky Business,* Financial Times/Prentice Hall.

Roddick, Anita (2005) *Business as Unusual: My Entrepreneurial Journey – Profits with Principles,* Anita Roddick Books.

Southon, Mike and West, Chris (2006) *The Beermat Entrepreneur: Turn Your Good Idea into a Great Business*, Prentice Hall.

Spain, Michael and Jackson, Liz (2005) *Start Up! How to Start a Successful Business from Absolutely Nothing, What To Do and How It Feels*, Prentice Hall.

Stutely, Richard (2006) *The Definitive Business Plan: The Fast Track for Executives and Entrepreneurs*, Financial Times/Prentice Hall.

Sugars, Bradley J. (2006) *Billionaire In Training: Build Businesses, Grow Enterprises, and Make Your Fortune (Instant Success)*, McGraw-Hill Professional.

Thompson, Geoff (2001) *The Great Escape: The 10 Secrets to Loving Your Life and Living Your Dreams*, Summersdale.

Thompson, Geoff (2006) *The Elephant and the Twig: The Art of Positive Thinking*, Summersdale.

Thompson, Geoff (2007) *Fear: The Friend of Exceptional People*, Summersdale.

Vise, David A. (2006) *The Google Story*, Pan Books.

Whyte, Stewart and Jess, Nigel (2006) *Starting and Running a B and B: A Practical Guide to Setting Up and Managing a Successful Bed and Breakfast Business*, How To Books.

Williams, Sara (2006) *The 'Financial Times' Guide to Business Start Up*, Financial Times/Prentice Hall.

Woodroffe, Simon (2000) *The Book of Yo!*, Capstone Publishing.

Woods, Caspian (2003) *From Acorns … How to Build Your Brilliant Business From Scratch*, Prentice Hall.

Index